THE LOWFAT GRILL

77 Surprisingly Succulent Recipes for Meats, Marinades, Vegetables, Sauces, and More!

DONNA RODNITZKY

PRIMA
PUBLISHING

Prima Publishing and colophon are trademarks of Prima Communications, Inc.

97 98 99 00 DD 10 9 8 7 6 5 4 3 2 1
Printed in the United States of America

HOW TO ORDER

Single copies of this book may be ordered from Prima Publishing, P.O. Box 1260BK, Rocklin, CA 95677, telephone (916) 632-4400. Quantity discounts are also available. On your letterhead, include information concerning the intended use of the books and the number of books you wish to purchase.

Visit us online at http://www.primapublishing.com

CONTENTS

PREFACE

THIS COOKBOOK IS ABOUT THE JOY OF INDULGING IN healthful cuisine that is delicious yet light and low in fat. It seems as though all the foods many of us enjoyed most when growing up were slathered with butter or deep-fried in cooking oil or shortening, but times have changed. Now that we understand more about healthful dining and appreciate the importance of limiting our fat intake, these mouth-watering morsels have become mere memories. Too often we are faced with the sad fact that the foods that taste best and rekindle the fondest memories are least healthful—and what better example of this dilemma than those wonderful meals prepared on an outdoor grill.

Whether a family picnic or a day at the beach with friends, who doesn't have a Pavlovian response to the memory of steaks or plump hamburgers sizzling on a barbecue grill, engulfed in an aromatic haze of charcoal smoke? As good as they taste, too many of these grilled treats contain more fat than is acceptable for a modern healthful diet. Does that mean we have to abandon this culinary tradition? Absolutely not! This book tells you how to limit the fat content of grilled foods while enhancing their natural flavors and preserving the smoky taste that is unique to grilling.

Let me explain how I met this challenge. My family and I realized that many grilled foods contain too much fat, but we didn't want to give up the wonderful ritual and taste of grilling. Grilling is not only a way of imparting a unique taste to foods, it is a happening–an escape from the kitchen and an opportunity to commune with nature (if only on the back porch or patio). For us, it was a family tradition. I had my marching orders. After much experimentation, I discovered the secret to tasty lowfat grilling.

You will be pleasantly surprised, as I was, that the marinades I developed for the leaner cuts of meat not only enhanced their flavor but tenderized them as well. Lean turkey is transformed into delicious turkey teriyaki, chicken breasts brim with the zestiness of lemon and pepper, and lean cuts of beef and vegetables combine in a grill-top wok to become a wonderful stir-fry. The smoky flavor from the grill mingling with the right spices, herbs, and sauces combine to make the simplest cut of meat a lowfat gourmet treat.

It is common knowledge that leaner cuts of meat are often less tender and less tasty and therefore not ideal for grilling. This cookbook, with its tenderizing and flavor-enhancing techniques, will allow you to use these less fatty cuts. Here are the lean cuts of meat you should choose for lowfat grilling:

Lean Cuts of Meat for Grilling

Beef	Pork	Lamb	Veal
round tip	tenderloin	loin chop	cutlet
top round	boneless top loin chop	leg	loin chop
eye of round	boneless ham, cured		
tenderloin	center loin of chop		
sirloin			

A useful rule of thumb is that the words "round" and "loin" signify lean beef and "loin" or "leg" imply lean pork. USDA "Select" beef is the leanest or has the least amount of marbling (these are the flecks of fat found within the meat), and "choice" is the second leanest. Keep in mind that these lean cuts of meat can be made even leaner by up to 50% just by removing any visible fat before cooking.

Grilling is also an ideal way to prepare seafood, and this book is full of recipes featuring a wide variety of ocean bounty. Just as with meats, combining seafood with the right seasoned vegetables and utilizing a flavorful marinade before grilling or a zesty sauce afterward results in a wonderful lowfat taste sensation that will satisfy the most demanding gourmet.

The majority of the recipes in the cookbook were tested on a kettle grill. However, most of the recipes can be adapted to a gas grill or almost any other type of grill. Depending on the heat and efficiency of your grill, cooking time may vary. Whatever technique, grill, or family secret you may possess for the perfect barbecue, this book will introduce you to an exciting new way to enjoy lighter cooking. Most of the recipes in this book can be started a day ahead and are quick and easy to prepare. A trip to an Asian food store will allow you to stock up on unique ingredients, and of course, substitutions are always possible. In fact, that is the beauty of these recipes. Just like chemistry, by combining a few key ingredients you can create a marvelous marinade that will allow the flavor in foods to come alive with a piquancy and zest that will surprise and please your family and guests.

I invite you to experience a world of wonderful flavors and to enjoy a more healthful lifestyle.

ACKNOWLEDGMENTS

This book would not have been possible without the cooperation and support of Prima Publishing. I would like to thank Acquisitions Editor, Alice Anderson; Project Editor, Susan Silva; Senior Project Editor, Steven Martin; Lindy Dunlavey, cover designer; and Bunny Martin, food stylist, for their efficiency and professionalism in guiding this book toward publication.

A special thank you goes to my husband, Bob, and my three children, David, Adam, and Laura who gave me their enthusiastic encouragement and support. Most of all, I appreciate their willingness to taste most of the recipes.

HELPFUL GUIDELINES

A WIDE VARIETY OF GRILLS IS AVAILABLE, EACH WITH unique characteristics. Some of the recipes in this cookbook were tested on a Weber Charcoal Kettle grill and others on a gas grill, but good results can be obtained with any of the popular grills described here.

GRILLS

Kettle grills

The kettle grill's hood and base are rounded so that heat is evenly reflected off of all surfaces and back onto the food. This makes cooking time shorter and locks in the natural flavors and juices of foods. Although the hood is removable, it is usually advisable to cook with it on. This limits the oxygen supply and prevents flare-ups, eliminating the need for water bottles and reducing the possibility of burning the food. Regulation of heat is controlled by vents on the base and hood, which should be in the open position when starting the charcoal and while cooking. However, if the heat from the coals becomes too great, the vents on the base can be closed. Make sure to use insulated barbecue mitts when adjusting the vents because they will be hot to the touch. Lastly, when the coals are cool, it is necessary to remove all accumulated ashes from the vents at the bottom of the grill to allow for proper ventilation with your next use.

Braziers or open grills

The open grill is most often made without a hood. It is round in shape, has a single cooking rack, and is supported on long legs. Some models are made with a half hood or wind screen. The brazier is an inexpensive way to grill, but its use should be limited to those foods that do not take a long time to prepare because the coals burn down to ashes very quickly. With this type of grill, it is useful to keep a water bottle nearby to extinguish any flare-ups that may occur when fat drips onto the coals.

Hooded grills

Hooded grills resemble kettle grills except they are square or rectangular and the hood is hinged onto the base. Food can be cooked either with the hood open as on a brazier or with it closed, allowing more smoke to accumulate and generating greater heat so that the food cooks faster.

Smoker

A smoker is an elongated, cylindrical grill. In addition to a fuel grate and a cooking rack, a pan is positioned between them. Water is added to this pan and when the liquid gets hot, it produces steam. Soaked, smoking wood chips of your choice are sprinkled on top of the hot coals. The combination of the steam from the hot water, cooking the food at a very low temperature, and smoke from the wood chips allows the food to acquire a very intense smoky flavor and at the same time remain moist and juicy. It may be necessary to add additional coals every 50 to 60 minutes, but avoid opening the lid unnecessarily as it may add to the cooking time.

Gas and electric grills

Gas and electric grills are very similar in design to a kettle or hooded grill. However, they use permanent lava rocks or ceramic briquette-shaped rocks instead of charcoal. These rocks are heated by an underlying gas burner or electric heating element. The major advantage of these grills is that they get hot quickly, and the briquettes do not have to be replaced since they do not burn down to ashes. A gas grill requires a gas canister or a natural gas hook-up; an electric grill requires a nearby electrical outlet. Both of these grills impart a smoky flavor when drippings from the food fall onto the hot briquettes and vaporize; however, the flavors are not nearly as intense as when charcoal is used.

LIGHTING COALS

When using a grill that requires charcoal, it is important to get all of the briquettes equally hot so that the food is uniformly cooked. The best way to accomplish this is to stack 20 to 30 coals in a pyramid before starting them on fire. There are several effective techniques to start the coals or fire as discussed below. After burning for 25 to 30 minutes, the coals should all be ashen gray on the outside and within the pyramid there should be a red glow. Using barbecue tongs, spread the coals out so they cover an area a little wider than the food to be cooked.

FIRE STARTERS

Chimney starter

The chimney is used to get coals hot in a short period of time. It is a metal cylinder with holes on the sides to allow for ventilation. It may have a wooden handle. The best way to use the chimney is to place some crumbled newspaper on the bottom of it and place coals on top. Open all the vents and set fire to the newspaper. In a very short time, the coals will be hot. Using the handle on the chimney, transfer the hot coals onto the fuel grate. If the chimney does not have a handle, be certain to use insulated barbecue mitts to transfer the hot coals.

Kindling

Take pieces of newspaper and roll them diagonally into a long, narrow cylinder. Grasp the ends and tie them into a knot. Place the knots in the bottom of the fuel grate and cover them with pieces of dry twigs or wood scraps. Loosely mound six to seven coals on top of the pile. Carefully ignite the newspaper knots. As coals ignite, add more coals to the mound, continuing this process until all the coals have been added. Using tongs, carefully spread out the coals over the fuel grate once they have become hot.

Electric starter

The electric starter consists of a heating element attached to an extended handle with a cord that plugs into an electrical outlet. The element is placed among the coals and when it is plugged in, it gets hot enough to ignite the coals resting on it. The hot coals ignite the others and, in time, all of the coals will become hot.

Block starters

Two to three of these small chemically treated cubes are placed among the coals and ignited with a match. They do not affect the taste of the food and are very easy to use.

Liquid starters

Liquid starters are a popular way to light coals. However, the chemicals in the starter are absorbed by the coals and can impart an unpleasant taste to your food. The best way to avoid this potential problem is to place only a few coals on the fuel grate and sprinkle them with starter. Add the remaining coals and ignite the treated coals. Using this technique, the majority of the coals are untreated and cannot generate a chemical taste. Never add additional starter if any of the coals are still burning as this practice is a serious fire hazard.

BRIQUETS AND WOOD CHIPS

Charcoal briquettes

Charcoal briquettes are made of carbonized scraps of wood, combined with a filler and compressed into the shape of a briquette. Often, chemicals are added that allow the coals to light more quickly. However, food cooked over these coals containing these additives can have an unpleasant taste. To minimize this problem, make sure all of the coals are uniformly ashen gray which indicates that the chemicals have completely burned away and are no longer a source of fumes.

Hardwood charcoal

Hardwood charcoal is made of wood without the addition of fillers or chemical additives, and therefore, does not give an unpleasant taste to grilled food. It burns hotter than ordinary charcoal briquettes. Charcoal of this type is frequently made of hickory, maple, oak, cherry, or mesquite.

Smoking chips or chunks

Smoking chips or chunks are used to impart a unique flavor to the food more so than to act as a fuel. They may be made of woods such as mesquite, cherry, alder, maple, hickory, oak, walnut, or apple, each having its own distinctive smoke aroma and flavor. Wood chips or chunks will generate the most smoke when allowed to sit in water for at least 30 minutes before they are scattered onto the hot coals. If you have any grape vines, they can also be used in the same way.

ACCESSORIES

There is no end to the number of accessories that have added new dimensions to creative grilling and at the same time, have made it so easy! All of the accessories described here or mentioned in the recipes are inexpensive; becoming a fully equipped grilling chef is relatively easy. On the other hand, you may find that with a little improvisation, cooking utensils you already own can be used for the same purpose.

Wire brush

This is an essential tool for keeping the grill clean. Each time you grill, the cooking rack should be scraped clean with a wire brush. This prevents food from sticking to the cooking rack and reduces the possibility of unpleasant flavors being added to the food.

Barbecue tongs

Tongs allow you to grasp foods without piercing them and allowing their natural juices to escape. They should be long enough so that your hand is at a safe distance from the area immediately above the hot grilling surface.

Grill wok

The grill wok is a four-sided metal basket with multiple symmetrical small holes all over the sides and bottom. It is placed directly on the cooking grate. A grill wok is invaluable for grill stir-frying because its high sides hold the food in place while stirring. Food cannot fall through the small holes, but smoke and grilling aromas pass through them easily.

Meat thermometer

The meat thermometer is an invaluable tool for determining the doneness (rare, medium, well-done) of steaks, roasts, pork, and poultry.

Grilling grid

The grid is a flat, porcelain grate with multiple holes symmetrically placed all over the bottom. Like the grill wok, it is placed directly on the cooking grate. It is excellent for cooking vegetables, or other foods that are too small or fragile to place over a conventional grate with widely spaced bars.

Drip pan

When a recipe calls for the indirect grilling method, a drip pan is placed at the center of the fuel grate, surrounded by charcoal briquettes. This arrangement allows the drippings from the foods to fall into the pan rather than on the coals which might cause flare-ups. You can make your own drip pan by folding two sheets of heavy duty aluminum foil into the shape of a pan.

Hinged wire basket

This accessory consists of two flat wire rectangular grids, hinged on one side. Food is placed between the wire grids and the two sides are closed, keeping the food in place. Adjustable hinged baskets are ideal for grilling hamburgers, fish, steaks, or other kinds of food that may be too fragile to turn.

Metal skewers

Metal skewers are perfect for making kebabs. They are very long and will hold a complete individual serving of meat or fish and vegetables. Unlike wooden skewers, these will not catch fire. Make sure to use an insulated barbecue mitt when touching them. If you use wooden skewers, soak them in water first for at least

30 minutes or overnight to reduce the chance of their catching fire.

Basting brushes

Basting brushes are ideal for brushing marinades or sauces onto food. Make sure to buy one with a long handle and of good quality—there is nothing worse than finding brush hairs on the food!

TECHNIQUES

When cooking with a grill, there are only two basic methods available: food is cooked directly or indirectly over the coals.

Direct method

The direct method is most frequently used when the food to be grilled can be cooked in 30 minutes or less. Using this technique, the food is placed on the cooking rack over the coals and is exposed directly to their heat.

Indirect method

The indirect method is used when the food to be grilled takes longer than 30 minutes to cook and when it is necessary to prevent the food from getting too close to the heat source. A drip pan is placed in the center of the fuel grate and an equal number of briquettes is placed on both sides. After the coals are ashen gray, the cooking grate is positioned over them and the food is placed directly over the drip pan rather than over the coals. If the cooking time is longer than 45 to 60 minutes, it may be necessary to add additional coals.

- Bring meat or fish to room temperature before grilling.

- To seal in the juices when grilling beef, sear it first by cooking it for one minute on each side. Test for doneness by inserting a meat thermometer to measure the temperature of the thickest part of the meat or by observing the color of the beef through a slit made near its center. If the thermometer registers 145 degrees, or if the center is deep pink and the outer portion is brown, then it is *medium rare*. A temperature of 160 degrees or a light pink center and brown outer portion, indicates that it is *medium*. A reading of 170 degrees or beef which appears uniformly brown throughout suggests that the meat is *well done*. For steaks, the best way to determine how long to cook the meat is to follow guidelines that relate to thickness. The Weber's Owner's Guide provides a useful chart for this purpose:

How Long to Cook Steak
(Cooking time in minutes)

	Rare		Medium		Well-Done	
	1st side	2nd side	1st side	2nd side	1st side	2nd side
1 inch thick	2	3	4	4	5	6
1½ inches thick	5	6	7	8	9	10
2 inches thick	7	8	9	9	10	11

- When cooking pork chops, sear the pork for 1 minute on each side. If the chop is ¾-inch thick, cook it for 4 to 5 minutes on each side; if 1½-inches thick, 8 to 10 minutes on each side. Although most recipes suggest cooking pork until a meat thermometer registers 160 degrees, I prefer to cook it until it registers 150 to 155 degrees, because at this temperature the meat is safely cooked but remains more tender and juicy.

• When a recipe calls for a butterflied leg of lamb, ask the butcher to remove the bone in the leg and spread the meat so it lays flat while grilling. The meat is done when a meat thermometer registers 150 degrees for medium-rare and 160 degrees for medium doneness.

• When grilling seafood, a good rule of thumb is that a ¾-inch piece of fish usually requires 8 minutes total cooking time and a 1-inch piece of fish requires 10 minutes or less. To check for doneness, insert a fork into the thickest part of the fish and determine if the flesh has become opaque and somewhat flaky. Remember that when fish is marinated in a sauce that contains lemon juice, the marinating time should be no more than 30 minutes. Otherwise, the lemon juice will initiate chemical changes in the fish similar to cooking.

• All of the chicken recipes in this book call for chicken breasts that are skinned, boned, and have all visible fat removed. When cooking chicken breasts on the grill, I like to turn them frequently to prevent burning and reduce drying. To determine doneness, prick the meat to see if it is white throughout and the juices run clear.

• Grilling time will be affected by the weather. Allow for more time in cold weather.

• When making kebabs, leave a small amount of space between portions of meat on the skewers to assure that each piece is cooked uniformly.

• It is best to coat the grill with a nonstick vegetable spray to prevent food from sticking to the grate. This should be done before the grate is placed over the heat.

• All vegetables should be coated with a cooking oil, preferably olive oil, before grilling as an additional measure to prevent them from sticking to the grill.

CHICKEN

4 SERVINGS

Balsamic vinegar gives the chicken a piquant flavor.

Marinade
¼ cup tamari
2 tablespoons balsamic vinegar
½ tablespoon extra-virgin olive oil
2 tablespoons minced fresh basil
½ teaspoon oregano
⅛ teaspoon freshly ground pepper
1 clove garlic, minced

2 chicken breasts (12 ounces each), skinned,
    boned, and halved

To make marinade
Combine tamari, balsamic vinegar, olive oil, basil, oregano, pepper, and garlic in nonmetal dish. Add chicken breasts and turn to coat both sides. Cover dish and refrigerate several hours or overnight, turning chicken at least once.

WHEN READY TO GRILL
Over hot coals, place chicken breasts on a grill coated with nonstick vegetable spray. Cover grill and cook 6 to 8 minutes, turning chicken every 3 minutes.

161 Calories
27.9 g Protein
1.6 g Carbohydrates
3.9 g Fat
22.0% Calories from Fat
0.0 g Fiber
567 mg Sodium
74 mg Cholesterol

4 SERVINGS

This is a fabulous way to enjoy New Orleans–style Cajun cooking without the usual worry about calories and fat. The spices add a marvelous zest to the chicken that is delicately balanced by the Lemon Dill Yogurt Sauce. Serve with mugs of chicken gumbo and a fresh fruit salad.

Cajun Spices

2 teaspoons paprika
$\frac{1}{4}$ teaspoon *each* cayenne and salt
$\frac{1}{8}$ teaspoon *each* freshly ground white pepper
    and black pepper, onion salt, garlic salt, thyme,
    and oregano

Lemon Dill Yogurt Sauce

1 cup plain nonfat yogurt
2 tablespoons fresh lemon juice
2 tablespoons finely chopped fresh dill
$\frac{1}{2}$ tablespoon extra-virgin olive oil
$\frac{1}{2}$ teaspoon sugar
2 cloves garlic, minced

Blackened Chicken

1 tablespoon fresh lemon juice
1 teaspoon extra-virgin olive oil
1 chicken breast (8 ounces), skinned and boned

4 pita pockets
2 tomatoes, thinly sliced
Shredded lettuce

239 Calories
17.4 g Protein
31.3 g Carbohydrates
5.0 g Fat
18.8% Calories from Fat
1.9 g Fiber
586 mg Sodium
26 mg Cholesterol

To make Cajun spices

Combine paprika, cayenne, salt, white pepper, black pepper, onion salt, garlic salt, thyme, and oregano in a small container and blend well. Set aside.

To make yogurt sauce

Combine yogurt, lemon juice, dill, olive oil, sugar, and garlic in a small bowl and blend well. Refrigerate, covered, for 1 to 2 hours.

To make chicken

Combine lemon juice and olive oil in a nonmetal dish. Add chicken and turn to coat both sides. Cover dish and refrigerate 20 minutes.

WHEN READY TO GRILL

Spread Cajun spices on a plate and coat both sides chicken breast in them. Over hot coals, place chicken breast on grill coated with nonstick vegetable spray. Cover grill and cook 6 to 8 minutes, turning chicken every 3 minutes. Allow chicken to come to room temperature before carving into thin slices.

WHEN READY TO SERVE

Warm pita according to package directions. Cut 1½ inches off one side of pita to make a pocket and fill with sliced chicken, tomatoes, and lettuce. Spoon a generous amount of Lemon Dill Yogurt Sauce over each sandwich.

4 SERVINGS

Grilled chicken was never so easy to make!
Serve with steamed string beans and Grilled Peaches.

Marinade

6 tablespoons Mango Vinaigrette*
3 tablespoons Honeycup prepared mustard

2 chicken breasts (12 ounces each), skinned,
  boned, and halved

To make marinade

Combine Mango Vinaigrette and mustard in a nonmetal
dish. Add chicken breasts and turn to coat both sides.
Cover dish and refrigerate several hours or overnight,
turning chicken breasts at least once.

WHEN READY TO GRILL

Over hot coals, place chicken breasts (reserve marinade)
on a grill coated with nonstick vegetable spray. Cover grill
and cook 6 to 8 minutes, turning chicken every 3 minutes
and brushing with marinade the last 3 minutes.

***Mango Vinaigrette is available at Williams-Sonoma, a food
specialty store located throughout the United States or through
their mail order catalog.**

169 Calories
26.9 g Protein
5.8 g Carbohydrates
3.7 g Fat
19.5% Calories from Fat
0.0 g Fiber
64 mg Sodium
74 mg Cholesterol

4 SERVINGS

The fusion of the mustards and tarragon produces a marvelous blend. It is used first to marinate the chicken breasts and later becomes the crowning touch when it is ladled over the grilled chicken. Serve with wheat pilaf and a fresh fruit salad.

Marinade

3 tablespoons *each* grainy mustard and Dijon mustard

3 tablespoons tarragon vinegar

1½ tablespoons extra-virgin olive oil

1½ tablespoons pineapple juice

¼ teaspoon freshly ground white pepper

2 chicken breasts (12 ounces each), skinned, boned, and halved

To make marinade

Combine mustards, tarragon vinegar, olive oil, pineapple juice, and white pepper in a nonmetal dish. Add chicken breasts and turn to coat both sides. Cover dish and refrigerate several hours or overnight, turning chicken at least once.

WHEN READY TO GRILL

Over hot coals, place chicken (reserve marinade) on a grill coated with nonstick vegetable spray. Cover grill and cook 6 to 8 minutes, turning chicken every 3 minutes.

While chicken is cooking, place reserved marinade in a small, heavy saucepan over moderately low heat and cook until it is heated through. Keep warm.

WHEN READY TO SERVE

Place chicken breasts on individual dinner plates. Spoon 1 to 2 tablespoonfuls of heated sauce over chicken and garnish each serving with a sprig of fresh parsley.

260 Calories
29.0 g Protein
6.1 g Carbohydrates
13.1 g Fat
45.4% Calories from Fat
0.0 g Fiber
577 mg Sodium
74 mg Cholesterol

4 SERVINGS

Raspberry-flavored grilled chicken and Raspberry Vinaigrette combine to make a colorful and refreshing salad to enjoy on a hot summer day.

Marinade

½ cup raspberry vinegar

2 tablespoons Dijon mustard

¼ teaspoon freshly ground white pepper

2 chicken breasts (10 ounces each), skinned, boned, and halved

Raspberry Vinaigrette

1 shallot (1 ounce), chopped

3 tablespoons raspberry vinegar

1 tablespoon Dijon mustard

⅛ teaspoon *each* salt and freshly ground white pepper

¼ cup extra-virgin olive oil

4 cups combined red leaf and romaine lettuce

2 pears, seeded and cut into wedges

Raspberries

318 Calories
24.0 g Protein
18.0 g Carbohydrates
17.6 g Fat
50% Calories from Fat
3.1 g Fiber
325 mg Sodium
61 mg Cholesterol

To make marinade

Combine raspberry vinegar, mustard, and white pepper in a nonmetal dish. Add chicken breasts and turn to coat both sides. Cover dish and refrigerate several hours or overnight, turning chicken at least once.

To make Raspberry Vinaigrette

In work bowl of food processor fitted with a metal blade, process shallot until finely chopped. Add raspberry vinegar, mustard, salt, and pepper and process until blended. Add olive oil in a slow steady stream and process until well blended. Set aside.

WHEN READY TO GRILL

Over hot coals, place chicken breasts on a grill coated with non-stick vegetable spray. Cover grill and cook 6 to 8 minutes, turning chicken every 3 minutes. Allow chicken to come to room temperature. When cool, carve the chicken into ¼-inch-thick slices.

WHEN READY TO SERVE

Divide lettuce among four salad plates. Place chicken on lettuce so it resembles an open fan, leaving spaces in between for slices of pears. Spoon 1½ to 2 tablespoons raspberry vinaigrette over each salad and garnish with fresh raspberries, if available.

6 SERVINGS

*Pizza cooked on a grill is a new taste sensation you will definitely enjoy!
It is at its best when flavored with an Asian sauce and topped with grilled
chicken and slivered red, orange, and yellow peppers.*

Sauce
½ cup hoisin sauce
1 teaspoon *each* teriyaki sauce, soy sauce, and
    Szechwan chili sauce*
½ teaspoon oyster sauce
1 teaspoon *each* minced garlic and fresh
    ginger root

1 chicken breast (12 ounces), skinned and boned

3 tandoori style naan* (Indian bread)
¾ cup shredded mozzarella cheese
6 tablespoons *each* slivered red, yellow, and
    orange pepper
¾ cup sliced fresh shiitake mushrooms
¾ cup shredded mozzarella cheese

***Szechwan chili sauce and Tandoori style naan are available
in most Asian or health food stores.**

327 Calories
23.8 g Protein
34.9 g Carbohydrates
10.4 g Fat
29% Calories from Fat
2.3 g Fiber
851 mg Sodium
41 mg Cholesterol

Prepare the grill by placing the charcoal on one half of the charcoal grate. This will enable you to move the pizza away from the heat source while it is cooking.

To make sauce

Combine hoisin sauce, teriyaki sauce, soy sauce, Szechwan chili sauce, oyster sauce, garlic, and ginger root in a small bowl.

WHEN READY TO GRILL

Brush both sides of the chicken breast with some of the sauce. Over hot coals, place chicken breast on a grill coated with nonstick vegetable spray. Cover grill and cook 6 to 8 minutes, turning chicken every 3 minutes. Allow chicken to cool for 5 minutes before cutting it into slivers.

To prepare pizzas

Brush remaining sauce on each piece of naan. Distribute ¼ cup mozzarella cheese over *each* naan and top each with peppers, mushrooms, grilled chicken slivers, and ¼ cup mozzarella cheese.

Place 1 to 2 pizzas (depending on the size of grill) over coals. Cover grill and cook 1 minute. Move pizza with tongs over to the side of grill where there are no coals. Continue to cook 10 minutes or until the cheese has melted. Remove pizza with a very wide spatula.

6 SERVINGS

The fusion of the smoky flavor of the chicken and the hot spices creates an exceptional chili. Depending on dietary restrictions, the chili is delicious topped either with fat-free or light shredded cheddar cheese and sour cream, in addition to chopped green onions and salsa.

½ pound small white beans
½ pound white northern beans
3 cans (14½ ounces each) fat-free chicken broth
1 large onion, chopped
4 cloves garlic, minced
1 yellow pepper, chopped
2 tablespoons chopped cilantro
1 tablespoon *each* cumin, oregano, and freshly
    ground white pepper
½ teaspoon coriander
¼ teaspoon salt
⅛ teaspoon cayenne

2 chicken breasts (12 ounces each), skinned
    and boned

1 can (4½ ounces), minced green chiles
2 tablespoons chopped banana pepper*

*Banana peppers are large, yellow peppers with a mild flavor.

381 Calories
43.2 g Protein
43.2 g Carbohydrates
4.1 g Fat
10% Calories from Fat
7.4 g Fiber
1247 mg Sodium
74 mg Cholesterol

Place beans in a large mixing bowl and add enough water to completely cover beans. Set aside for 24 hours.

Drain beans and rinse well. Place beans in a Dutch oven and add 2 cans chicken broth, onion, garlic, yellow pepper, cilantro, cumin, oregano, white pepper, coriander, salt, and cayenne. Bring to a boil over moderate heat. Lower heat, cover, and simmer 4 hours, adding more chicken broth, if necessary. While chili is cooking, grill the chicken breasts.

When the chili has cooked for 4 hours, add the grilled chicken cubes, remaining chicken broth, green chiles, and banana pepper and blend well. Taste for seasoning. Cover and cook an additional 1 hour. The chili can be served immediately or allowed to sit in the refrigerator for 24 hours to let the flavors blend.

WHEN READY TO GRILL
Over hot coals, place chicken breasts on a grill coated with non-stick vegetable spray. Cover grill and cook 6 to 8 minutes, turning chicken every 3 minutes. Allow the chicken to cool for 10 minutes. Cut the chicken into 1-inch cubes and set aside.

4 SERVINGS

*This delicious dish is a cornucopia of colors and textures. The marinade
is sensational and would also be great in combination with pork or turkey.
Serve with wheat pilaf and a combination of green beans and mandarin oranges.*

Marinade

½ cup *each* tamari and rice wine

2 tablespoons *each* fresh lemon juice and honey

2 tablespoons toasted sesame seeds

½ tablespoon extra-virgin olive oil

1 teaspoon sesame oil

1 teaspoon dry mustard

½ teaspoon freshly ground pepper

2 dashes hot pepper sauce

2 cloves garlic, minced

1 piece fresh ginger root, peeled and cut
¼ inch thick

2 chicken breasts (12 ounces each), skinned,
boned, and cut into 1½-inch cubes

Kebab Vegetables

8 mushroom caps

1 yellow pepper, cut into eight 1½-inch pieces

4 green onions, each cut into two 2-inch lengths

8 cherry tomatoes

270 Calories
31.3 g Protein
19.7 g Carbohydrates
5.9 g Fat
20% Calories from Fat
2.5 g Fiber
1080 mg Sodium
74 mg Cholesterol

To make marinade

Combine tamari, rice wine, lemon juice, honey, sesame seeds, olive oil, sesame oil, mustard, pepper, hot pepper sauce, garlic, and ginger root in a nonmetal dish. Add chicken cubes and turn to evenly coat. Cover dish and refrigerate several hours or overnight, turning chicken at least once.

WHEN READY TO GRILL

Alternate pieces of chicken, mushrooms, yellow pepper, green onions, and tomatoes on skewers. Over hot coals, place skewers on a grill coated with nonstick vegetable spray. Cover grill and cook 6 to 8 minutes, turning chicken every 3 minutes.

---

4 SERVINGS

Tandoori chicken is an Indian dish traditionally baked in a special oven (tandoor); however, this recipe has been altered so it can be made on an ordinary grill. The chicken is very spicy and hot. Serve with an Indian vegetable dish, yogurt, and naan, a tender Indian flat bread available in most Asian food stores.

WHEN READY TO GRILL

Over hot coals, place chicken breasts on a grill coated with non-stick vegetable spray. Cover grill and cook 6 to 8 minutes, turning every 3 minutes.

160 Calories
28.0 g Protein
3.0 g Carbohydrates
3.3 g Fat
19% Calories from Fat
0.3 g Fiber
209 mg Sodium
74 mg Cholesterol

Marinade

5 cloves garlic
1 tablespoon minced fresh ginger root
2 tablespoons fresh lemon juice
1 tablespoon garam masala*
1 teaspoon cayenne
½ teaspoon *each* paprika and salt
¼ teaspoon saffron
½ cup plain nonfat yogurt

2 chicken breasts (12 ounces each), skinned, boned, and halved

In work bowl of food processor fitted with a metal blade, process garlic and ginger root until finely chopped. Add lemon juice, garam masala, cayenne, paprika, salt, and saffron and process until smooth. Add yogurt and process just to blend. Transfer yogurt mixture to a nonmetal dish. Place chicken breasts in marinade and turn chicken to coat both sides. Cover dish and refrigerate several hours or overnight.

*Garam masala is available in most Asian food stores. To make your own: combine 1 tablespoon *each* ground cardamom and cinnamon, 1 teaspoon *each* ground cloves, cayenne, and cumin, ¼ teaspoon *each* mace and ground nutmeg in a small container and mix well. Store in a tightly closed container.

TURKEY

4 SERVINGS

The selection of turkey cuts now available makes it easy to enjoy this lowfat meat in a variety of interesting and delicious ways. Serve this quick and easy turkey entree with wheat pilaf and grilled Pineapple Rings.

Marinade

¼ cup soy sauce
2 tablespoons honey
1 clove garlic, minced
1 piece fresh ginger root, peeled and sliced
   ½ inch thick
⅛ teaspoon hot pepper sauce

1 turkey breast (1 pound), cut into ¾-inch cubes
1 green pepper, cut into ¼-inch slices
1 cup thinly sliced mushrooms
1½ cups fresh pineapple chunks

To make marinade

Combine soy sauce, honey, garlic, ginger root, and hot pepper sauce in a nonmetal dish. Add turkey and toss to coat pieces. Cover dish and refrigerate several hours.

While turkey is cooking, add vegetable mixture to reserved marinade and blend well.

Add vegetables, pineapple, and marinade to wok and stir-fry for 1 minute. Cover grill and cook 2 minutes.

WHEN READY TO GRILL

Over hot coals, place a grilling wok that has been coated with non-stick vegetable spray. Add turkey (reserve marinade and discard ginger root) and stir-fry for 1 minute. Cover grill and cook 2 minutes. Repeat stir fry and cooking process one more time.

211 Calories
26.9 g Protein
19.1 g Carbohydrates
3.1 g Fat
13% Calories from Fat
1.2 g Fiber
1085 mg Sodium
58 mg Cholesterol

4 SERVINGS

The zesty marinade makes the turkey exceptionally juicy and flavorful. Serve with Cranberry Chutney, sweet potatoes, and a combination of peas and small onions.

Cranberry Chutney

1 cup sugar
1 cup cold water
½ cup chopped onions
4 whole cloves
1 teaspoon cinnamon
½ teaspoon salt
¼ cup distilled white vinegar
2 cups fresh or frozen cranberries
½ cup raisins
½ cup chopped dried dates
¼ cup chopped preserved ginger
¼ cup firmly packed dark brown sugar

Marinade

1 tablespoon Dijon mustard
1½ tablespoons extra-virgin olive oil
1 teaspoon thyme
½ teaspoon *each* salt, pepper, poultry seasoning, savory, and sage
¼ teaspoon paprika

1 fresh turkey breast (3 pounds), split

392 Calories
55.1 g Protein
21.5 g Carbohydrates
8.8 g Fat
20.3% Calories from Fat
2.0 g Fiber
370 mg Sodium
126 mg Cholesterol

*The nutritional analysis is based on using ¼ cup of chutney per serving.

To make Cranberry Chutney:

Combine sugar, water, onions, cloves, cinnamon, salt, and vinegar in a medium-size saucepan over moderate heat. Bring to boil and simmer 5 minutes. Add cranberries, raisins, dates, ginger, and brown sugar and blend well. Simmer 10 to 12 minutes. Remove saucepan from heat and bring to room temperature. Refrigerate cranberry chutney in a covered container.

To make marinade

Combine mustard, olive oil, thyme, salt, pepper, poultry seasoning, savory, sage, and paprika in a small bowl. Rub mixture over top of turkey.

WHEN READY TO GRILL

Prepare a grill with a drip pan in the center of the lower grate and place an equal number of briquettes on both sides. When coals are hot, place the turkey centered over the drip pan on a grill coated with a nonstick vegetable spray. Cover grill and cook 2 to 2½ hours, or until turkey is no longer pink inside when a knife is inserted into the thickest part and a meat thermometer registers 170 degrees.

4 SERVINGS

*The marinade is a masterful balance of Asian flavorings. It can be used
with pork or chicken, but it goes exceptionally well with turkey.
Serve with mango muffins and a salad of mixed baby greens.*

WHEN READY TO GRILL
Over hot coals, place turkey (reserve marinade) on a grill coated with nonstick vegetable spray. Cover grill and cook 6 to 8 minutes, turning turkey every 3 minutes and brushing with marinade.

242 Calories
37.9 g Protein
6.5 g Carbohydrates
6.3 g Fat
23.3% Calories from Fat
0.1 g Fiber
436 mg Sodium
86 mg Cholesterol

Marinade
½ cup pineapple juice
2 tablespoons soy sauce
2 tablespoons Honeycup prepared mustard
1 tablespoon *each* extra-virgin olive oil, honey, and hoisin sauce
½ tablespoon oyster sauce
½ teaspoon sesame oil
⅛ teaspoon Chinese Five Spice powder
1 piece fresh ginger root, sliced ¼ inch thick and peeled

1½ pounds turkey tenderloins

To make marinade
Combine pineapple juice, soy sauce, mustard, olive oil, honey, hoisin sauce, oyster sauce, sesame oil, Chinese Five Spice powder, and ginger root in a large nonmetal dish. Set aside.

Divide turkey tenderloins into four pieces. Using a meat mallet, pound each tenderloin until it is ½ inch thick. Place tenderloins in marinade and turn to coat both sides. Cover dish and refrigerate several hours or overnight, turning turkey at least once.

4 SERVINGS

*The peppercorn mustard has a wonderful, piquant taste that
intensifies the flavor of the turkey. Serve these colorful kebabs with
Grilled Yams and steamed julienne vegetables.*

Marinade

6 tablespoons fresh lemon juice

3 tablespoons Grey Poupon peppercorn mustard

½ tablespoon extra-virgin olive oil

¾ teaspoon freshly ground pepper

3 cloves garlic, minced

1½ pounds turkey tenderloin, cut into
   1¼-inch cubes

Kebab Vegetables

1 green pepper, cut into eight 1-inch squares

8 mushrooms

8 cherry tomatoes

1 yellow squash, cut into eight ¼-inch slices

To make marinade

Combine lemon juice, mustard, olive oil, pepper, and
garlic in a nonmetal dish. Add cubed turkey and turn
to coat pieces. Cover dish and refrigerate several hours
or overnight, turning turkey at least once.

WHEN READY TO GRILL

Alternate pieces of
turkey, pepper, mush-
rooms, tomatoes, and
squash on metal skew-
ers. Over hot coals,
place kebabs on a grill
coated with nonstick
vegetable spray. Cover
grill and cook 6 to 8
minutes, turning every
3 minutes.

250 Calories

39.6 g Protein

9.0 g Carbohydrates

6.0 g Fat

22% Calories from Fat

1.9 g Fiber

239 mg Sodium

86 mg Cholesterol

TURKEY HOT DOGS

8 SERVINGS

This is the kind of food my children like to prepare when their friends come over in the afternoon. They grill the onions, green peppers, banana peppers, and roma tomatoes in a grilling wok and place the hot dogs on the grate. The grilled vegetables along with relish, sauerkraut, and yellow mustard garnish the hot dogs and turn this everyday fare into a gourmet delight!

WHEN READY TO SERVE
Place a hot dog in each bun and garnish each serving with grilled vegetables and favorite condiments.

8 banana peppers
1 large onion, thinly sliced
1 red pepper, thinly sliced
8 roma tomatoes, halved

8 turkey hot dogs (97% fat free)
8 whole wheat turkey buns

WHEN READY TO GRILL
Over hot coals, place banana peppers on a grill. Cover grill and cook peppers 4 minutes on each side, or until skins are charred all over. Place peppers in a plastic bag for 15 minutes. When the peppers are cool enough to handle, peel away the skin and remove the top and seeds. Cut the peppers in half and set aside.

Place onions, red pepper, and tomatoes in a grilling wok coated with nonstick vegetable spray. Cover grill and cook 10 to 12 minutes, turning vegetables every 3 minutes. During the last 8 minutes of cooking time, place the hot dogs alongside the wok on the grill and cook 8 minutes or until brown, turning frequently.

232 Calories
12.6 g Protein
34.3 g Carbohydrates
4.7 g Fat
19% Calories from Fat
4.9 g Fiber
780 mg Sodium
20 mg Cholesterol

8 SERVINGS

This is a wonderful way to prepare turkey burgers! The marinade enhances the flavor of the turkey and the toppings add crunch and color. Serve with corn on the cob and a fresh fruit salad.

2 cloves garlic, minced
3 pieces nonfat bread
2 pounds ground turkey tenderloin
⅓ cup pineapple juice
¼ cup soy sauce
2 teaspoons honey
¼ teaspoon powdered ginger

8 whole wheat hamburger buns
½ cup chutney
8 green pepper slices, cut ¼ inch thick
8 pineapple slices, cut ¼ inch thick
8 green onions, cut in half

In work bowl of food processor fitted with a metal blade, process garlic until finely chopped. Add bread and process until finely chopped. Combine ground turkey, bread mixture, pineapple juice, soy sauce, honey, and ginger in a small bowl and blend well. Cover dish and refrigerate several hours.

WHEN READY TO GRILL
Form turkey into eight patties. Over hot coals, place patties on a grilling grid coated with nonstick vegetable spray. Cover grill and cook 5 to 7 minutes on each side.

WHEN READY TO SERVE
Place each burger on bottom half of a hamburger bun and top with 1 tablespoon chutney, a green pepper slice, a pineapple slice, and 2 pieces of green onion that form an X on top, and the top half of the bun.

384 Calories
30.9 g Protein
49.7 g Carbohydrates
6.2 g Fat
15% Calories from Fat
4.7 g Fiber
884 mg Sodium
58 mg Cholesterol

6 SERVINGS

*The spinach, herbs, and apricot preserves add a special
flavor to these turkey burgers. They are delicious topped with
grilled onions or a combination of fresh pineapple slices, onion, and green
pepper slices. Serve with corn on the cob and a cold pasta salad.*

1½ pounds ground turkey
1½ cups packed fresh spinach, washed, dried,
    and cut into small pieces
1 cup minced onions
½ cup whole wheat bread crumbs
¼ cup chopped parsley
2 tablespoons apricot preserves
1 teaspoon freshly ground pepper
¼ teaspoon salt

Combine turkey, spinach, onions, bread crumbs,
parsley, apricot preserves, pepper, and salt in a large
bowl and blend well. Cover bowl and refrigerate several hours.

WHEN READY TO GRILL
Form turkey mixture into six patties. Over hot coals, place
burgers on a grilling grid coated with nonstick vegetable
spray. Cover grill and cook 9 to 11 minutes, turning burgers every 3 minutes.

255 Calories
22.1 g Protein
13.6 g Carbohydrates
12.0 g Fat
42% Calories from Fat
1.1 g Fiber
230 mg Sodium
58 mg Cholesterol

4 SERVINGS

Satay is an Indonesian specialty featuring slices of marinated chicken or beef grilled and served with a peanut dipping sauce. In this recipe using turkey instead, the marinade and dipping sauce are one and the same.

Marinade

3 cloves garlic, minced

6 tablespoons reduced-fat creamy peanut butter

3 tablespoons soy sauce

2 tablespoons fresh lime juice

1 tablespoon red Thai curry paste

2 tablespoons minced fresh basil

1½ tablespoons extra-virgin olive oil

1½ tablespoons orange marmalade

¼ teaspoon curry powder

1½ pounds turkey tenderloin, cut into
    1½-inch cubes

To make marinade

In work bowl of food processor fitted with metal blade, process garlic until finely chopped. Add peanut butter, soy sauce, lime juice, red curry paste, basil, olive oil, marmalade, and curry; process until smooth.

Transfer marinade to a nonmetal dish and add turkey cubes; toss to coat pieces. Cover dish and refrigerate several hours or overnight.

WHEN READY TO GRILL

Place turkey cubes (reserve marinade) on skewers, leaving a small amount of space between pieces. Over hot coals, place turkey on a grill coated with nonstick vegetable spray. Cover grill and cook 6 to 8 minutes, turning kebabs every 3 minutes. Serve the reserved marinade as a dipping sauce for the turkey.

419 Calories

45.1 g Protein

17.5 g Carbohydrates

18.2 g Fat

39.1% Calories from Fat

1.2 g Fiber

1069 mg Sodium

86 mg Cholesterol

TURKEY TENDERLOINS WITH BARBECUE GLAZE

4 SERVINGS

The flavor of the turkey is deliciously enhanced with this zesty marinade. Serve with Grilled Yams and steamed broccoli.

Marinade

2 tablespoons *each* tarragon vinegar, honey, and
    hoisin sauce
½ tablespoon *each* extra-virgin olive oil and
    Worcestershire sauce
1 teaspoon Dijon mustard
⅛ teaspoon *each* salt, crushed red pepper, and
    freshly ground pepper
1 clove garlic, minced

1½ pounds turkey tenderloin

To make marinade

Combine vinegar, honey, hoisin sauce, olive oil, Worcestershire sauce, mustard, salt, red pepper, black pepper, and garlic in a nonmetal dish. Set aside.

Divide turkey tenderloins into four pieces. Using a meat mallet, pound each tenderloin until it is slightly less than ½ inch thick. Place turkey in marinade and turn to coat both sides. Cover dish and refrigerate several hours or overnight, turning turkey at least once.

WHEN READY TO GRILL

Over hot coals, place turkey (reserve marinade) on a grill coated with nonstick vegetable spray. Cover grill and cook 6 to 8 minutes, turning turkey every 3 minutes and brushing with marinade the last 6 minutes of cooking time.

229 Calories
37.7 g Protein
6.0 g Carbohydrates
5.1 g Fat
20% Calories from Fat
0.1 g Fiber
251 mg Sodium
86 mg Cholesterol

4 SERVINGS

The intense flavor of sun-dried tomatoes enhances the taste of the yogurt marinade. The marinade pairs well with the turkey and keeps it tender and juicy during the grilling process.

Marinade

6 sun-dried tomatoes packed in oil, drained
   and minced
6 tablespoons plain nonfat yogurt
3 tablespoons Dijon mustard
¼ teaspoon *each* salt, crushed red pepper, and
   freshly ground pepper

4 turkey tenderloins (6 ounces each)

To make marinade

Combine tomatoes, yogurt, mustard, salt, crushed red pepper, and black pepper in a nonmetal dish. Set aside.

Using a meat mallet, pound each tenderloin until it is slightly less than ½ inch thick. Place turkey in marinade and turn to coat both sides. Cover dish and refrigerate several hours or overnight, turning turkey at least once.

WHEN READY TO GRILL

Over hot coals, place tenderloins on a grill coated with nonstick vegetable spray. Cover grill and cook 6 to 8 minutes, turning turkey every 3 minutes.

221 Calories
38.5 g Protein
3.6 g Carbohydrates
4.8 g Fat
20% Calories from Fat
0.6 g Fiber
310 mg Sodium
86 mg Cholesterol

BEEF

BEEF FAJITAS

6 SERVINGS

Fajitas are a very popular Tex-Mex dish. After the beef is grilled, it is served in tortillas and customarily topped with an array of condiments, most of which are high in fat. Serve this healthful version, using carefully substituted lowfat ingredients instead.

Marinade

¼ cup fresh lime juice
½ teaspoon *each* lemon pepper and garlic salt

1 beef round (1 pound), thinly sliced

1 green pepper, thinly sliced
1 medium onion, thinly sliced
6 soft flour tortillas (warmed according to
  package directions)
6 tablespoons fat-free cheddar cheese
6 tablespoons lowfat sour cream
6 tablespoons salsa

To make marinade

Combine lime juice, lemon pepper, and garlic salt in a nonmetal dish. Add beef and blend well. Cover dish and refrigerate several hours or overnight.

WHEN READY TO GRILL

Over hot coals, place green pepper and onion slices in a grilling wok coated with nonstick vegetable spray. Cover grill and cook vegetables 10 to 12 minute, or until brown and soft, turning every 4 minutes. Remove green peppers and onions to a bowl and keep warm.

Add beef to grilling wok and cook, covered, 8 to 10 minutes, or until meat is no longer pink, turning every 4 minutes.

WHEN READY TO SERVE

Divide beef and grilled pepper and onions among six warmed tortillas. Top with one tablespoon *each* cheese, sour cream, and salsa.

262 Calories
23.6 g Protein
22.8 g Carbohydrates
8.2 g Fat
28% Calories from Fat
1.8 g Fiber
310 mg Sodium
55 mg Cholesterol

BEEF TENDERLOIN WITH MUSTARD SAUCE

6 SERVINGS

*The flavor of the beef is greatly enhanced by the Mustard Sauce.
Serve with wild rice, steamed julienne vegetables, and a tossed salad.*

WHEN READY TO SERVE
Spoon 2 tablespoons of warm Mustard Sauce on individual dinner plates. Place a filet on the sauce and garnish each serving with a sprig of parsley.

Marinade
2 tablespoons Dijon mustard
1 tablespoon *each* yellow and grainy mustard
3 tablespoons tarragon vinegar
1½ tablespoons pineapple juice
1½ tablespoons extra-virgin olive oil
¼ teaspoon freshly ground white pepper

6 beef tenderloin filets (5 ounces each)
salt and pepper
parsley

To make Mustard Sauce
Combine mustards, vinegar, pineapple juice, olive oil, and white pepper in a small heavy saucepan over moderately low heat and cook until heated through, stirring occasionally. Keep warm.

WHEN READY TO GRILL
Slightly flatten beef filets and lightly sprinkle both sides with salt and pepper. Over hot coals, place filets on a grill coated with nonstick vegetable spray. Cover grill and cook 4 minutes on each side or until a meat thermometer registers 145°.

292 Calories
33.2 g Protein
2.6 g Carbohydrates
15.8 g Fat
49% Calories from Fat
0.0 g Fiber
285 mg Sodium
96 mg Cholesterol

4 SERVINGS

These hamburgers are delicious served as they are on a whole wheat bun or topped with thinly sliced tomatoes, onions, red pepper rings, and lettuce.

2 pieces nonfat bread
1½ pounds (90% lean) ground round beef
¼ cup Grey Poupon peppercorn mustard
¼ cup minced parsley
4 cloves garlic, minced
2 teaspoons Worcestershire sauce
1 teaspoon freshly ground pepper
¼ teaspoon salt

In work bowl of food processor fitted with a metal blade, process bread into fine bread crumbs. Combine bread crumbs, beef, mustard, parsley, garlic, Worcestershire sauce, pepper, and salt in a large bowl and blend well. Cover bowl and refrigerate several hours. Form beef into six patties.

WHEN READY TO GRILL
Over hot coals, place hamburgers on a grill coated with nonstick vegetable spray. Cover grill and cook 4 to 5 minutes on each side.

452 Calories
39.5 g Protein
12.0 g Carbohydrates
26.2 g Fat
52% Calories from Fat
0.6 g Fiber
763 mg Sodium
121 mg Cholesterol

6 SERVINGS

Marinating a sirloin steak in this wonderful combination of sauces intensifies the flavor imparted by the grilling smoke and keeps the meat juicy. Serve with corn on the cob and your favorite tossed salad.

WHEN READY TO GRILL

Over hot coals, place steak on a grill coated with nonstick vegetable spray. Sear steak for 1 minute on each side. Cover grill and cook steak 4 to 6 minutes on each side, or until a meat thermometer registers 155 to 160°. Allow steak to sit 5 minutes before carving it into thin slices.

302 Calories
41.6 g Protein
3.0 g Carbohydrates
12.9 g Fat
38.4% Calories from Fat
0.1 g Fiber
351 mg Sodium
122 mg Cholesterol

Marinade

¼ cup ketchup

2 tablespoons *each* white wine and soy sauce

1 tablespoon *each* balsamic vinegar and
   steak sauce

½ tablespoon *each* honey, Worcestershire sauce,
   and extra-virgin olive oil

¼ teaspoon *each* thyme and freshly
   ground pepper

1 sirloin tip steak (2¼ pounds), all visible
   fat removed

To make marinade

Combine ketchup, wine, soy sauce, vinegar, steak sauce, honey, Worcestershire sauce, olive oil, thyme, and pepper in a nonmetal dish (or a 1-gallon reclosable plastic bag). Add steak and turn to coat both sides. Cover dish and refrigerate several hours or overnight, turning steak at least once.

GRILLED STEAKS IN TAMARI MARINADE

4 SERVINGS

The marinade is a cornucopia of flavors that helps create an exceptionally delicious and juicy steak. Serve with your favorite soup and a tossed salad.

Marinade
¼ cup *each* tamari and white wine vinegar
1 tablespoon *each* extra-virgin olive oil,
    Worcestershire sauce, and fresh lemon juice
1 tablespoon dry mustard
1 teaspoon freshly ground pepper
¼ teaspoon salt
2 cloves garlic, minced

1 top loin sirloin steak (1½ pounds), all visible
    fat removed

To make marinade
Combine tamari, vinegar, olive oil, Worcestershire sauce, lemon juice, dry mustard, pepper, salt, and garlic in a nonmetal dish (or 1-gallon reclosable plastic bag). Add steak and turn to coat both sides. Cover dish and refrigerate several hours or overnight, turning steak at least once.

WHEN READY TO GRILL
Over hot coals, place steak on a grill coated with nonstick vegetable spray. Sear steak for 1 minute on each side. Cover grill and cook 4 to 6 minutes on each side, or until a meat thermometer registers 155 to 160°. Allow steak to sit 5 minutes before carving into thin slices.

313 Calories
42.6 g Protein
2.2 g Carbohydrates
14.3 g Fat
41.2% Calories from Fat
0.0 g Fiber
678 mg Sodium
122 mg Cholesterol

4 SERVINGS

The marinade has an Asian flavor, and it adds a wonderful essence to the London broil. It is especially flavorful and colorful with the roasted pepper slices. Serve with spaghetti squash and Grilled Vegetable Kebabs.

Marinade

2 tablespoons *each* soy sauce and rice vinegar
1 tablespoon *each* dry sherry and honey
1 tablespoon fresh lemon juice
½ teaspoon sesame oil
½ teaspoon dry mustard
¼ teaspoon crushed red pepper
2 cloves garlic, minced
1 piece fresh ginger root, peeled and cut
    ¼ inch thick

1 London broil (1½ pounds)

2 large red peppers

To make marinade

Combine soy sauce, rice vinegar, sherry, honey, lemon juice, sesame oil, mustard, crushed red pepper, garlic, and ginger root in a nonmetal dish (or a 1-gallon reclosable plastic bag). Add London broil and turn to coat both sides. Cover dish and refrigerate overnight, turning beef occasionally.

315 Calories
40.4 g Protein
7.9 g Carbohydrates
12.3 g Fat
35.2% Calories from Fat
0.3 g Fiber
749 mg Sodium
105 mg Cholesterol

WHEN READY TO GRILL

Over hot coals, place the red peppers on a grill. Cover grill and cook 14 to 20 minutes, or until skins are charred all over, turning peppers as skins blacken. Place the peppers in a plastic bag for 15 minutes. When peppers are cool enough to handle, peel away the skin and remove the top and seeds (do not rinse the peppers). Cut peppers into thin strips and set aside.

Place London broil on grill. Sear steak for 1 minute on each side. Cover grill and cook 4 to 6 minutes on each side, or until a meat thermometer registers 155 to 160°, brushing beef with marinade occasionally.

WHEN READY TO SERVE

Carve London broil into very thin slices, cutting against grain. Arrange sliced beef on individual dinner plates and garnish each serving with red pepper strips.

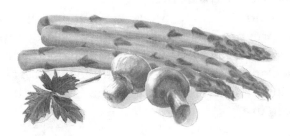

4 SERVINGS

*This salad is a light and refreshing meal to enjoy on a
hot summer day. The beef and dressing can be prepared ahead and the
rest of the salad combined at the last minute. Serve with cut-up fresh melons.*

Oriental Salad Dressing
1½ teaspoons chopped fresh ginger root
1 small garlic clove
½ cup rice vinegar
1 tablespoon *each* extra-virgin olive oil and tamari
1 tablespoon sugar
¼ teaspoon *each* crushed red pepper and salt

1 pound beef tenderloin, thinly sliced

Salad
3 cups sliced bok choy
2 cups bean sprouts
3 green onions, thinly sliced
1 small red pepper, thinly sliced
1 small yellow pepper, thinly sliced
1 tablespoon sesame seeds

289 Calories
30.0 g Protein
12.7 g Carbohydrates
13.6 g Fat
42.3% Calories from Fat
2.0 g Fiber
485 mg Sodium
77 mg Cholesterol

To make Oriental Salad Dressing
In work bowl of food processor fitted with a metal
blade, process ginger root and garlic until chopped.
Add rice vinegar, olive oil, tamari, sugar, crushed red
pepper, and salt and process until blended. Transfer
dressing to a covered container and refrigerate until
ready to use.

WHEN READY TO GRILL

Over hot coals, place beef tenderloin in a grilling wok coated with nonstick vegetable spray. Cover grill and cook 4 to 6 minutes, or just until beef is no longer pink, turning every 2 minutes. Transfer beef to a bowl and pour 1 to 2 tablespoons Oriental Salad Dressing over beef and turn to coat all over. Refrigerate, covered, until ready to use.

WHEN READY TO SERVE

Combine bok choy, bean sprouts, onions, red and yellow peppers, sesame seeds, and beef in a large salad bowl. Add Oriental Salad Dressing and toss to blend well. Divide the salad among four dinner plates.

4 SERVINGS

This colorful salsa is a sensational combination of southwestern flavors and textures. Serve this entree with a baked potato with lowfat or fat-free sour cream and a hefty scoop of the Gazpacho Salsa.

Marinade
¼ cup fresh lime juice
1 teaspoon extra-virgin olive oil
3 cloves garlic, minced
½ teaspoon *each* cumin, cayenne, and
   chili powder
¼ teaspoon freshly ground pepper

1½ pounds top sirloin steak, all visible
   fat removed

Gazpacho Salsa
½ cup *each* diced red and yellow pepper
½ cup *each* diced red onion and tomato
2 cloves garlic, minced
2 jalapeños, seeded and diced*
2 tablespoons cilantro, finely chopped
1 tablespoon extra-virgin olive oil
½ tablespoon sherry vinegar

*The seeds of jalapeño peppers are very hot. To avoid burning your skin, wear rubber or latex gloves when removing the seeds. Immediately wash the knife, cutting surface, and gloves when finished.

359 Calories
43.3 g Protein
9.0 g Carbohydrates
16.7 g Fat
41.8% Calories from Fat
1.7 g Fiber
98 mg Sodium
123 mg Cholesterol

To make marinade

Combine lime juice, olive oil, garlic, cumin, cayenne, chili powder, and pepper in a nonmetal dish (or a 1-gallon reclosable plastic bag). Add steak and turn to coat both sides. Cover dish and refrigerate several hours or overnight, turning steak at least once.

To make Gazpacho Salsa

Combine red and yellow peppers, onions, tomatoes, garlic, jalapeños, cilantro, olive oil, and sherry vinegar in a medium bowl and blend well. Refrigerate, covered, until ready to serve. Makes 2 cups.

WHEN READY TO GRILL

Over hot coals, place steak on grill coated with nonstick vegetable spray. Sear steak for 1 minute on each side. Cover grill and cook 4 to 6 minutes on each side or until a meat thermometer registers 155 to 160°. Allow steak to sit for 5 minutes.

WHEN READY TO SERVE

Carve steak into thin slices and either spoon some of the Gazpacho Salsa over the top or place it beside the steak.

4 SERVINGS

*This recipe can be made with less beef and more broccoli and onions
to further reduce the fat and calories. Serve with steamed basmati rice.*

Marinade
1 tablespoon cold water
½ tablespoon soy sauce
1 teaspoon sugar
1 piece fresh ginger root, peeled and sliced
   ½ inch thick

½ pound beef tenderloin, thinly sliced

Sauce
2 tablespoons oyster sauce
½ tablespoon *each* rice wine and soy sauce
1 teaspoon sugar

2½ cups broccoli florets
8 green onions, cut into 2-inch pieces

159 Calories
18.0 g Protein
12.6 g Carbohydrates
4.6 g Fat
25.8% Calories from Fat
3.6 g Fiber
623 mg Sodium
38 mg Cholesterol

To make marinade

Combine water, soy sauce, sugar, and ginger root in a nonmetal dish. Add beef and toss to coat the pieces. Cover dish and refrigerate 1 hour.

To make sauce

Combine oyster sauce, rice wine, soy sauce, and sugar and blend well. Set aside.

Cook broccoli in a large pot of boiling water for 30 seconds. Rinse under cold water and drain well.

WHEN READY TO GRILL

Over hot coals, place beef in a grilling wok coated with nonstick vegetable spray. Cover grill and cook 2 minutes. Stir-fry beef for 30 seconds. Cover grill and cook 2 more minutes. Remove beef to a serving dish and set aside. Add broccoli and green onions to wok and stir-fry 1 minute. Cover grill and cook 2 minutes. Add beef and sauce and stir-fry until heated through.

4 SERVINGS

Hearty red wine combined with the tamari and spices in the marinade infuses the beef with a rich flavor and tenderizes it.

Marinade
¼ cup red wine
1 tablespoon tamari
½ tablespoon extra-virgin olive oil
¼ teaspoon *each* salt and freshly ground pepper
⅛ teaspoon hot pepper sauce
1 clove garlic, minced

1 beef tenderloin (1½ pounds)

To make marinade
Combine wine, tamari, olive oil, salt, pepper, hot pepper sauce, and garlic in a nonmetal dish (or a 1-gallon reclosable plastic bag). Add beef tenderloin and turn to coat both sides. Cover dish and refrigerate several hours or overnight.

WHEN READY TO GRILL
Prepare a grill with a drip pan in the center of the lower grate and place an equal number of briquettes on both sides of pan. When the coals are hot, place beef tenderloin over coals on a grill coated with nonstick vegetable spray. Sear the beef for 1 minute on each side. Move the beef with tongs directly over the drip pan. Cover grill and cook beef for 40 to 50 minutes, or until a meat thermometer registers 150°. Allow the beef tenderloin to sit for 5 minutes before carving it into thin slices.

297 Calories
39.2 g Protein
0.5 g Carbohydrates
13.9 g Fat
42.0% Calories from Fat
0.0 g Fiber
286 mg Sodium
115 mg Cholesterol

LAMB

8 SERVINGS

*The combination of mustard, herbs, and lemon adds a robust flavor
to the lamb. Serve with Grilled Vegetable Kebabs and fresh pasta.*

Marinade
¼ cup fresh lemon juice
3 tablespoons red wine vinegar
2 tablespoons extra-virgin olive oil
1 tablespoon Dijon mustard
1 tablespoon freshly ground pepper
1 teaspoon rosemary
½ teaspoon salt
¼ teaspoon crushed red pepper
4 cloves garlic, minced

1 leg of lamb (3 pounds), butterflied

Combine lemon juice, vinegar, olive oil, mustard, pepper, rosemary, salt, red pepper, and garlic in a large
nonmetal dish (or 1-gallon reclosable plastic bag).
Add lamb and turn to coat both sides. Cover dish and
refrigerate several hours or overnight, turning lamb at
least once.

WHEN READY TO GRILL
Over hot coals, place lamb on a grill coated with nonstick
vegetable spray. Sear the lamb for 1 minute on each side.
Cover grill and cook 25 to 30 minutes, or until a meat thermometer registers 150° for medium-rare or 160° for
medium, turning lamb every 8 minutes. Remove lamb from
grill and allow to sit 5 minutes before carving it into thin
slices.

319 Calories
35.2 g Protein
1.2 g Carbohydrates
18.4 g Fat
52.0% Calories from Fat
0.0 g Fiber
177 mg Sodium
120 mg Cholesterol

4 SERVINGS

*The flavor of the lamb is highlighted by the combination of fresh herbs in this marinade.
Serve with a Greek Salad and rice pilaf mixed with raisins and toasted pine nuts.*

Marinade
¼ cup *each* dry white wine and fresh lemon juice
1½ tablespoons extra-virgin olive oil
3 cloves garlic, minced
2 tablespoons *each* chopped parsley, dill, and
　　green onions
1 teaspoon oregano

1 leg of lamb (1½ pounds), butterflied

Greek Salad
Dressing
¼ cup red wine vinegar
¾ teaspoon *each* dry mustard and oregano
¼ teaspoon *each* salt and sugar
⅛ teaspoon freshly ground pepper
½ teaspoon minced garlic
¼ teaspoon fresh lemon juice
¾ cup extra-virgin olive oil

365 Calories
35.5 g Protein
3.0 g Carbohydrates
21.7 g Fat
53.6% Calories from Fat
0.3 g Fiber
90 mg Sodium
120 mg Cholesterol

1 small head escarole, torn into bite-size pieces
1 small head romaine lettuce, torn into bite-size
　　pieces
1 large tomato, cut into 8 wedges
1 small Spanish onion, thinly sliced
1 green pepper, thinly sliced
8 Greek olives (*kalamatas*)

8 Greek peppers (*peperoncini*)
¼ pound feta cheese, crumbled
4 anchovy filets
2 hard-boiled eggs, each cut into 4 wedges

To make marinade

Combine wine, lemon juice, olive oil, garlic, parsley, dill, green onions, and oregano in a 1-gallon reclosable plastic bag. Add lamb and turn to coat both sides. Seal the bag and place in the refrigerator for several hours or overnight, turning lamb at least once.

To make Greek Salad Dressing

Combine vinegar, mustard, oregano, salt, sugar, pepper, garlic, and lemon juice in work bowl of a food processor fitted with a metal blade and process until blended. In a slow steady stream, add olive oil and process until smooth. (The dressing can be made ahead and stored in the refrigerator in a covered container.)

Combine escarole, romaine lettuce, tomato, onion, and green pepper in a large bowl. Add enough dressing to coat the salad; toss well. Divide the salad among four salad plates and top each serving with 2 Greek olives, 2 Greek peppers, feta cheese, 1 anchovy filet, and 2 wedges of hard-boiled egg. (The lettuce, tomatoes, onions, and green peppers can be prepared a few hours ahead and stored in reclosable plastic bags in the refrigerator.)

WHEN READY TO GRILL

Over hot coals, place lamb (reserve marinade) on a grill coated with nonstick vegetable spray. Sear the lamb for 1 minute on each side. Cover grill and cook 25 to 30 minutes, or until a meat thermometer registers 150° for medium-rare or 160° for medium, turning lamb every 8 minutes. Baste with reserved marinade the last 15 minutes of cooking time. Allow lamb to sit for 5 minutes before carving it into thin slices.

4 SERVINGS

*Gyro sandwiches are very popular throughout the Middle East.
The leg of lamb is often cooked on a spit and thinly sliced or ground lamb is
combined with spices, formed into meat balls, and cooked on the grill.
The sandwiches are especially delicious when topped with Yogurt Sauce.*

Yogurt Sauce
¾ cup plain nonfat yogurt
5 tablespoons chopped cucumber
3 tablespoons chopped Bermuda onion
¼ teaspoon *each* garlic powder and freshly
   ground white pepper

1½ pounds ground leg of lamb
2 tablespoons oregano
1½ tablespoons *each* garlic powder and
   onion powder
¾ tablespoon freshly ground pepper
½ teaspoon thyme
¼ teaspoon salt

4 whole wheat pitas, cut in half
1 small onion, thinly sliced
1 small tomato, thinly sliced

590 Calories
43.2 g Protein
38.7 g Carbohydrates
28.6 g Fat
43.7% Calories from Fat
4.7 g Fiber
544 mg Sodium
129 mg Cholesterol

To make Yogurt Sauce

Combine yogurt, cucumber, onion, garlic powder, and white pepper in a small bowl. Cover bowl and refrigerate for several hours.

Combine lamb, oregano, 1½ tablespoons garlic powder, onion powder, pepper, thyme, and salt in a medium bowl and blend well. Make lamb into patties by forming 2 tablespoons of lamb mixture into a ball and flattening each one with your hands.

WHEN READY TO GRILL

Over hot coals, place lamb patties on a grilling grid coated with nonstick vegetable spray. Cover grill and cook 4 to 5 minutes on each side.

WHEN READY TO SERVE

Place three lamb patties into warmed pita half. Top each serving with Yogurt Sauce, sliced onions, and tomatoes.

6 SERVINGS

The contrast of the spicy lamb and the subtle flavor of vegetables coated with chili oil is sensational. Serve the lamb kebabs on a bed of Mediterranean Rice Pilaf and accompany it with Raita (page 58).

Kebab Vegetables

1 tablespoon chili oil

6 cauliflower florets, parboiled 5 minutes

6 new potatoes, halved and parboiled 18 minutes

2 large carrots, cut into six 2-inch chunks, parboiled 6 minutes

Marinade

1 cup plain low fat yogurt

2 cloves garlic, minced

1 tablespoon fresh lemon juice

1 teaspoon curry powder

¼ teaspoon *each* garam masala*, salt, coriander, and powdered ginger

⅛ teaspoon crushed red pepper

1 boneless leg of lamb (1½ pounds), cut into 1½-inch cubes

Mediterranean Rice Pilaf

4½ tablespoons light margarine

⅓ cup chopped onions

1½ cups long-grain rice

3 cups fat-free chicken broth

1 cup dried apricots, diced

1 cup raisins

1 tablespoon sugar

¼ teaspoon cinnamon

¼ cup toasted almond slivers

*Garam masala is available in most Asian food stores.

To make marinade

Combine yogurt, garlic, lemon juice, curry powder, garam masala, salt, coriander, ginger, and red pepper in a nonmetal dish (or a 1-gallon reclosable plastic bag). Add lamb and toss to coat all of the pieces. Cover dish and refrigerate for several hours or overnight.

To make Mediterranean Rice Pilaf

Melt 2 tablespoons of the margarine in a large frying pan over medium-high heat. Add onions and sauté until translucent. Add rice and cook until golden. Add chicken broth, bring to a boil, and simmer over low heat for 25 minutes.

While rice is cooking, melt the other 2½ tablespoons margarine in large skillet over medium heat. Add apricots, raisins, and sugar and stir until evenly coated. Cook 3 to 5 minutes or until heated through, stirring frequently. Add cinnamon, almonds, and cooked rice and blend well.

WHEN READY TO GRILL

Pour chili oil into a plastic bag and add vegetables. Roll vegetables in oil to coat pieces. Alternate pieces of lamb with vegetables onto metal skewers. Over hot coals, place skewers on a grill coated with nonstick vegetable spray. Cover grill and cook 8 to 10 minutes, turning kebabs every 4 minutes.

352 Calories
28.1 g Protein
28.7 g Carbohydrates
13.6 g Fat
34.8% Calories from Fat
5.2 g Fiber
196 mg Sodium
81 mg Cholesterol

8 SERVINGS

The profusion of herbs, mustard, and sauces in the marinade intensifies the flavor of the lamb. Serve with Grilled Ratatouille.

WHEN READY TO GRILL

Over hot coals, place lamb on a grill coated with nonstick vegetable spray. Sear the lamb for 1 minute on each side. Cover grill and cook 25 to 30 minutes, or until a meat thermometer registers 150° for medium-rare and 160° for medium, turning lamb every 8 minutes. Allow lamb to sit for 5 minutes before carving it into thin slices.

329 Calories
36.0 g Protein
4.2 g Carbohydrates
17.9 g Fat
48.9% Calories from Fat
0.4 g Fiber
738 mg Sodium
120 mg Cholesterol

Marinade

½ cup *each* soy sauce and red wine vinegar
¼ cup Worcestershire sauce
¼ cup Grey Poupon peppercorn mustard
1 tablespoon extra-virgin olive oil
2 bay leaves
2 teaspoons rosemary
½ teaspoon freshly ground pepper
¼ teaspoon *each* thyme and marjoram
1 medium onion, thinly sliced
4 cloves garlic, minced

1 leg of lamb (3 pounds), butterflied

To make marinade

Combine soy sauce, vinegar, Worcestershire sauce, mustard, olive oil, bay leaves, rosemary, pepper, thyme, marjoram, onion, and garlic in a nonmetal dish (or a 1-gallon reclosable plastic bag). Add lamb and turn to coat both sides. Cover dish and refrigerate for several hours or overnight, turning lamb at least once.

4 SERVINGS

These lamb meatballs are overflowing with the flavor of spices and herbs. They are delicious stuffed in pita bread and topped with grilled onions, diced tomatoes, and Raita (page 58).

2 pounds lean ground lamb
1 cup minced cilantro
½ cup finely minced Bermuda onion
4 cloves garlic
½ teaspoon *each* cayenne, coriander, cumin, paprika, and freshly ground pepper
¼ teaspoon salt

4 whole wheat pita breads
1 tomato, thinly sliced
1 onion, thinly sliced
2 tablespoons Raita

In a medium bowl, combine lamb, cilantro, onion, garlic, cayenne, coriander, cumin, paprika, pepper, and salt and blend well. Form mixture into 12 meatballs and place them on skewers.

WHEN READY TO GRILL
Over hot coals, place the meatballs on a grill coated with nonstick vegetable spray. Cover grill and cook 8 to 10 minutes, turning lamb every 3 minutes.

WHEN READY TO SERVE
Prepare pita bread according to manufacturer's instructions. Cut about 1½ to 2 inches off one side of pita to make a pocket. Place 3 meatballs in each and top with sliced tomatoes, grilled onion slices, and Raita.

696 Calories
52.5 g Protein
35.3 g Carbohydrates
37.3 g Fat
48.2% Calories from Fat
5.3 g Fiber
592 mg Sodium
171 mg Cholesterol

4 SERVINGS

*These spicy lamb meatballs can either be served as an
entree with rice pilaf and Raita or as a sandwich when warmed pita
bread is filled with the Koftas and topped with Raita.*

Raita

2 cups plain low fat yogurt
2 cucumbers, peeled and grated
1 medium onion, finely chopped
½ teaspoon cumin
¼ teaspoon salt

Koftas

2 slices nonfat white bread
2 tablespoons chopped onion
3 tablespoons chopped parsley
1 pound ground lamb
½ teaspoon *each* cinnamon and powdered ginger
¼ teaspoon *each* cardamom, allspice, crushed
   red pepper, salt and freshly ground pepper
⅛ teaspoon *each* mace, nutmeg, and cloves
1 medium egg

1 green pepper, cut into eight 1-inch squares
8 cherry tomatoes

443 Calories
33.7 g Protein
31.2 g Carbohydrates
20.0 g Fat
40.7% Calories from Fat
4.0 g Fiber
553 mg Sodium
141 mg Cholesterol

To make Raita

Fit a fine-sieved strainer over another strainer and place it over a large bowl. Spoon yogurt into strainer. Place grated cucumbers in a medium bowl. Allow yogurt and cucumbers to sit at room temperature for 1 hour.

Remove cucumbers from bowl and place in a strainer. Discard the liquid from the cucumbers and yogurt. Combine the yogurt, cucumber, onion, cumin, and salt in a medium bowl and blend well. Refrigerate, covered, for several hours.

To make Koftas

In work bowl of food processor fitted with metal blade, process bread into fine bread crumbs. Add onion and parsley and process until finely chopped.

In a large mixing bowl, combine lamb with bread mixture, cinnamon, ginger, cardamom, allspice, red pepper, salt, pepper, mace, nutmeg, cloves, and egg and blend well.

WHEN READY TO GRILL

Form 2 tablespoons lamb mixture into meatballs. Alternate meatballs with green pepper and tomatoes on skewers. Over hot coals, place skewers on a grill coated with nonstick vegetable spray. Cover grill, cooking 8 to 10 minutes, turning lamb frequently.

4 SERVINGS

The Asian marinade and smoky flavor from the grill combine to make a sensational, highly spiced and flavorful lamb and vegetable stir-fry. Serve with steamed basmati rice.

Marinade

2 tablespoons *each* hoisin sauce, water, and plum sauce

1 tablespoon *each* rice wine, soy sauce, Szechwan chili sauce, and honey

1 piece fresh ginger root, peeled and cut ¼ inch thick

1 tablespoon minced garlic

1 boneless leg of lamb (1 pound), thinly sliced into 1-inch strips

1½ cups broccoli florets, parboiled 1 minute

1 red pepper, cut into ⅛-inch strips

1 yellow pepper, cut into ⅛-inch strips

½ cup shiitake mushrooms, sliced

4 green onions, cut into 2-inch lengths

323 Calories
27.8 g Protein
24.5 g Carbohydrates
11.6 g Fat
32.3% Calories from Fat
3.5 g Fiber
583 mg Sodium
80 mg Cholesterol

To make marinade

Combine hoisin sauce, water, plum sauce, rice wine, soy sauce, Szechwan chili sauce, honey, ginger root, and garlic in a nonmetal dish (or a 1-gallon reclosable plastic bag). Add lamb and turn to coat all over. Cover dish and refrigerate for several hours or overnight, turning lamb at least once.

WHEN READY TO GRILL

Over hot coals, place lamb (reserve marinade and discard ginger root) in a grilling wok coated with nonstick vegetable spray on a grill. Stir-fry lamb for 1 minute. Cover grill and cook 2 minutes. Remove cover and stir-fry lamb 1 minute. Add broccoli, red and yellow peppers, shiitake mushrooms, and green onions; stir-fry 1 minute. Cover grill and cook 2 minutes. Transfer lamb and vegetables to a large serving bowl and add reserved marinade; blend well.

6 SERVINGS

The Iowa City Press Citizen *had a wonderful article on the joy of grilling. Wine-Basted Lamb Kebabs was a featured recipe, and it comes from the people who know everything about lamb, the Benton and Iowa County, Iowa, Sheep Producers Association.*

WHEN READY TO GRILL
Over hot coals, place kebabs 4 inches from heat for 8 to 10 minutes, turning frequently. Brush with sauce in the final minutes of cooking.

1½ pounds leg of lamb, cut into 1-inch cubes
24 Chinese pea pods
24 cherry tomatoes
24 pineapple chunks
½ cup chili sauce
½ cup brown sugar
½ cup red wine
2 tablespoons lemon juice
1 tablespoon dry mustard
½ teaspoon salt

Thread 12 skewers with a lamb cube, pea pod, cherry tomato, and pineapple. Repeat, ending with lamb.

In small saucepan, combine chili sauce, brown sugar, red wine, lemon juice, mustard, and salt. Bring to a boil, stirring until smooth. Remove from heat.

379 Calories
26.3 g Protein
39.3 g Carbohydrates
12.0 g Fat
28.5% Calories from Fat
3.3 g Fiber
524 mg Sodium
80 mg Cholesterol

PORK

4 SERVINGS

This is a delicious way to prepare pork chops. It is quick and easy and is certain to be a favorite among the younger set!

Barbecue Sauce

¼ cup barbecue sauce
3 tablespoons peach jam
2 tablespoons horseradish
½ tablespoon Dijon mustard

4 butterfly pork chops (6 ounces each), cut
  ¾ inch thick

To make Barbecue Sauce

Combine barbecue sauce, peach jam, horseradish, and mustard in a small bowl.

WHEN READY TO GRILL

Over hot coals, place pork chops on a grill coated with nonstick vegetable spray. Sear pork chops for 1 minute on each side. Brush pork chops with half of the sauce and cook 4 to 5 minutes. Turn pork chops over and brush with remaining sauce; cook 4 to 5 minutes or until a meat thermometer registers 155°.

369 Calories
42.2 g Protein
15.7 g Carbohydrates
14.3 g Fat
34.8% Calories from Fat
0.2 g Fiber
407 mg Sodium
129 mg Cholesterol

6 SERVINGS

The Asian flavors in the marinade and smoky taste from the grill blend well with pork. Serve with Fruit Kebabs and steamed pea pods.

Marinade
¼ cup tamari
3 tablespoons rice wine
2 tablespoons *each* rice vinegar and honey
1 tablespoon kecap manis*
2 cloves garlic, minced
⅛ teaspoon Chinese Five Spice powder

1 pork tenderloin (2¼ pounds), all visible
   fat removed

To make marinade
Combine tamari, rice wine, rice vinegar, honey, kecap manis, garlic, and Chinese Five Spice powder in a non-metal dish (or a 1-gallon reclosable plastic bag). Add pork tenderloin and turn to coat both sides. Cover dish and refrigerate several hours or overnight, turning pork at least once.

WHEN READY TO GRILL
Over hot coals, place pork tenderloin (reserve marinade) on a grill coated with nonstick vegetable spray. Sear the pork for 1 minute on each side. Cover grill and cook 15 to 18 minutes, or until a meat thermometer registers 150 to 155°, turning pork every 5 minutes and basting with marinade the last 6 minutes of cooking time. Allow pork to sit for 5 minutes before carving it into thin slices.

*Kecap manis is an Indonesian condiment found in most Asian food stores.

222 Calories
34.0 g Protein
6.8 g Carbohydrates
5.6 g Fat
22.6% Calories from Fat
0.0 g Fiber
465 mg Sodium
107 mg Cholesterol

4 SERVINGS

The fabulous balance of the kecap manis (sweet soy sauce) and honey with the garlic and crushed red pepper in this marinade elevates pork tenderloin to a gourmet experience. The marinade would also enhance the flavor of lamb or chicken. Serve with rice and Fruit Kebabs.

Marinade
¼ cup *each* honey mustard and kecap manis*
1 tablespoon rice vinegar
2 large cloves garlic, minced
⅛ teaspoon crushed red pepper

1 pork tenderloin (1½ pounds)

To make marinade
Combine honey mustard, kecap manis, rice vinegar, garlic, and red pepper in a nonmetal dish (or a 1-gallon reclosable plastic bag). Add pork tenderloin and turn to coat all over. Cover dish and refrigerate several hours or overnight.

WHEN READY TO GRILL
Prepare a grill with a drip pan in the center of the lower grate and place an equal number of briquettes on both sides of pan. When coals are hot, place pork (reserve marinade) directly over drip pan and cook, covered, 20 to 25 minutes, or until a meat thermometer registers 150° to 155°, turning pork occasionally and brushing with reserved marinade the last 10 minutes of cooking time. Allow pork to sit for 5 minutes before carving it into thin slices.

*Kecap manis is an Indonesian condiment found in most Asian food stores.

234 Calories
33.5 g Protein
14.0 g Carbohydrates
5.8 g Fat
22.4% Calories from Fat
0.0 g Fiber
427 mg Sodium
107 mg Cholesterol

6 SERVINGS

Not only do these pork chops taste delicious, but the flavorful sauce spooned over each one is appealing to the eye.

Marinade
¾ cup soy sauce
1 cup pineapple juice
½ cup currant jelly
¼ cup honey
2 tablespoons *each* Dijon mustard and fresh
    lemon juice
¼ teaspoon Worcestershire sauce
1 piece fresh ginger root, peeled and cut
    ¼ inch thick
2 cloves garlic, minced

6 pork top loin chops (6 ounces each), cut
    ¾ inch thick

412 Calories
37.0 g Protein
38.3 g Carbohydrates
12.0 g Fat
26.3% Calories from Fat
0.1 g Fiber
2283 mg Sodium
107 mg Cholesterol

To make marinade

Combine soy sauce, pineapple juice, jelly, honey, mustard, lemon juice, Worcestershire sauce, ginger root, and garlic in a measuring pitcher and blend well. Pour half of the marinade in a nonmetal dish. Add pork chops and turn to coat both sides. Cover dish and refrigerate several hours or overnight, turning pork chops at least once. Refrigerate remaining marinade in a covered container to use as a sauce for the cooked pork chops.

WHEN READY TO GRILL

Over hot coals, place pork chops on a grill coated with nonstick vegetable spray. Sear pork chops for 1 minute on each side. Cover grill and cook 4 to 5 minutes on each side or until a meat thermometer registers 155°.

While the pork chops are cooking, heat the reserved marinade in a small saucepan over moderate heat. Bring to a boil and cook over moderately high heat for 12 to 14 minutes, or until sauce is reduced to 3/4 cup. Remove ginger root. Keep sauce warm over very low heat.

WHEN READY TO SERVE

Spoon 2 tablespoons sauce over top of each pork chop and garnish with a fresh sprig of parsley.

4 SERVINGS

*This smoke-flavored pork tenderloin is delicious accompanied
by Cranberry Chutney (page 20), squash, and a salad of mixed greens tossed
with a raspberry vinaigrette.*

Marinade

2 tablespoons bourbon

1 tablespoon molasses

1 tablespoon *each* fresh lemon juice and
extra-virgin olive oil

3 cloves garlic, minced

1 teaspoon thyme

½ teaspoon crushed red pepper

1 pork tenderloin (1½ pounds), all visible
fat removed

302 Calories
33.5 g Protein
3.9 g Carbohydrates
9.0 g Fat
26.7% Calories from Fat
0.1 g Fiber
84 mg Sodium
107 mg Cholesterol

To make marinade

Combine bourbon, molasses, lemon juice, olive oil, garlic, thyme, and red pepper in a nonmetal dish (or a 1-gallon reclosable plastic bag). Add pork and turn to coat both sides. Cover dish and refrigerate several hours or overnight, turning pork at least once.

WHEN READY TO GRILL

While briquettes are getting hot, soak 1 cup smoking wood chips according to package instructions. When the coals are ready, sprinkle the wet chips over them. Place the pork tenderloin (reserve marinade) over the hot coals and sear it for 1 minute on each side. Cover grill and cook 15 to 18 minutes or until a meat thermometer registers 150 to 155°, turning pork every 5 minutes and brushing with reserved marinade the last 6 minutes of cooking time. Allow pork tenderloin to sit for 5 minutes before carving it into thin slices.

MONGOLIAN PORK ROAST WITH GINGER-PINEAPPLE SAUCE

4 SERVINGS

The simplicity of pork roast is impressively transformed into a gourmet treat by the exotic flavors in the marinade, further complemented by the unusual combination of pineapple, apples, and fresh ginger in the sauce. Serve with sautéed new potatoes.

Marinade

¼ cup hoisin sauce

1 teaspoon *each* teriyaki sauce and rice wine

1 teaspoon minced garlic

1 piece fresh ginger root, peeled and cut
   ¼ inch thick

1 boneless loin pork roast (1½ pounds), all visible
   fat removed

Ginger-Pineapple Sauce

1½ cups fresh pineapple, cubed

2 Delicious apples, peeled, seeded, and cubed

¼ cup sugar

½ cup water

1 tablespoon fresh lemon juice

½ ounce fresh ginger root, peeled and cut
   into sticks

1 3-inch cinnamon stick

350 Calories
35.6 g Protein
11.6 g Carbohydrates
17.1 g Fat
44.0% Calories from Fat
0.9 g Fiber
536 mg Sodium
91 mg Cholesterol

To make marinade

Combine hoisin sauce, teriyaki sauce, rice wine, garlic, and ginger root in a nonmetal dish (or a 1-gallon reclosable plastic bag). Add pork roast and turn to coat both sides. Cover dish and refrigerate several hours or overnight, turning pork at least once.

To make Ginger-Pineapple Sauce

Combine pineapple, apples, sugar, water, lemon juice, ginger root, and cinnamon stick in a medium saucepan over moderate heat and bring to a boil. Reduce heat, cover, and simmer 20 minutes. Remove cinnamon and ginger. Transfer sauce to work bowl of food processor fitted with a metal blade and puree. Spoon sauce into covered container and refrigerate several hours or overnight.

WHEN READY TO GRILL

Over hot coals, place pork roast on a grill coated with nonstick vegetable spray. Sear the pork roast for 1 minute on each side. Cover grill and cook 40 to 45 minutes, or until a meat thermometer registers 150 to 155°, turning pork every 5 minutes. Allow pork roast to sit for 5 minutes before carving it into thin slices.

WHEN READY TO SERVE

Divide the pork among four dinner plates. Accompany each serving with Ginger-Pineapple Sauce on the side.

4 SERVINGS

*This orange marmalade marinade not only glazes the pork roast
as it cooks but imbues it with a deliciously rich flavor and keeps it moist
and juicy. Serve with Grilled Yams and a mixed green salad.*

Marinade
¼ cup orange marmalade
2 tablespoons *each* Dijon mustard and reduced-fat
   creamy peanut butter
1 tablespoon fresh lemon juice
½ tablespoon extra-virgin olive oil
1 teaspoon white horseradish
⅛ teaspoon *each* salt and freshly ground pepper

1 boneless loin pork roast (1½ pounds)

To make marinade
Combine orange marmalade, Dijon mustard, peanut
butter, lemon juice, olive oil, horseradish, salt, and pepper in a nonmetal dish (or a 1-gallon reclosable plastic
bag). Add pork roast and turn to coat both sides. Cover
dish and refrigerate several hours or overnight, turning pork at least once.

WHEN READY TO GRILL
Over hot coals, place pork roast (reserve marinade) on a
grill coated with nonstick vegetable spray. Sear the pork
roast for 1 minute on each side. Cover grill and cook 18 to
22 minutes or until a meat thermometer registers 150 to
155°, turning pork every 5 minutes and brushing with reserved marinade after pork has cooked for 12 minutes.
Allow pork roast to sit for 5 minutes before carving it into
thin slices.

425 Calories
36.8 g Protein
16.2 g Carbohydrates
22.2 g Fat
47.1% Calories from Fat
0.4 g Fiber
401 mg Sodium
91 mg Cholesterol

PORK CHOPS WITH DILL SAUCE

*The intensity of the fresh dill in the sauce highlights the flavor
of the pork. I like to marinate the pork chops in half the sauce and
save the remainder to spoon over them once they are cooked. The leftover pork
can also be thinly sliced and stuffed into a whole wheat pita pocket with thinly sliced
tomatoes and sweet onions topped with alfalfa sprouts for a great snack or lunch.*

Dill Sauce

6 tablespoons *each* Grey Poupon peppercorn
   mustard and fresh lemon juice
¼ cup lowfat plain yogurt
3 tablespoons chopped fresh dill
½ teaspoon freshly ground pepper

4 butterfly pork chops (6 ounces each), cut
   1 inch thick

To make Dill Sauce

Combine mustard, lemon juice, yogurt, dill, and pepper in a nonmetal dish. Remove ½ cup Dill Sauce and refrigerate, covered, until ready to serve. Add pork chops to dish and turn to coat both sides. Cover dish and refrigerate several hours or overnight.

WHEN READY TO GRILL

Over hot coals, place pork chops on a grill coated with nonstick vegetable spray. Sear the pork chops for 1 minute on each side. Cover grill and cook 6 to 8 minutes on each side or until a meat thermometer registers 155°.

WHEN READY TO SERVE

Divide chops among four dinner plates and spoon 2 tablespoons of the reserved dill sauce over each one. Garnish each serving with a sprig of fresh dill, if desired.

329 Calories
43.2 g Protein
2.5 g Carbohydrates
15.2 g Fat
41.7% Calories from Fat
0.0 g Fiber
408 mg Sodium
129 mg Cholesterol

6 SERVINGS

*Slices of pork with prune and apple filling covered with
red currant sauce are spectacular to look at and wonderful to eat.
Serve with a sweet potato and carrot puree and grilled Apple Rings.*

6 to 8 bite-size prunes
3 tablespoons Madeira

1 pork boneless loin roast (2 pounds), all visible
  fat removed
1 small apple, cubed
½ teaspoon salt
¼ teaspoon freshly ground pepper
2 tablespoons Madeira

Currant Sauce
¾ cup currant jelly
1 tablespoon dry mustard
1 tablespoon Madeira

402 Calories
30.8 g Protein
34.0 g Carbohydrates
15.1 g Fat
33.7% Calories from Fat
1.0 g Fiber
262 mg Sodium
81 mg Cholesterol

Place prunes in a small nonmetal dish and cover with 3 tablespoons Madeira. Cover dish and allow it to sit for several hours or overnight.

Using a sharp knife, make a hole in the center of each end of the pork roast. Push the handle of a wooden spoon through entire length of roast, turning to make a tunnel approximately ½ inch in diameter. Alternately stuff prunes (reserve Madeira) and apple cubes into tunnel, pushing from both ends. Sew openings shut at both ends with poultry lacer or large needle and heavy thread. Place roast in a nonmetal dish and sprinkle with salt and pepper. Pour 2 more tablespoons Madeira along with the reserved Madeira over roast. Cover dish and refrigerate several hours.

WHEN READY TO GRILL

Prepare a grill with a drip pan in the center of the lower grate and place an equal number of briquettes on both sides of the pan. When coals are hot, place the pork roast (reserve the marinade) over the coals on a grill coated with nonstick vegetable spray. Sear the pork for 1 minute on each side. Move the pork directly over the drip pan. Cover grill and cook 1 hour and 15 minutes, or until a meat thermometer registers 150 to 155°, brushing occasionally with reserved marinade.

To make Currant Sauce

While the pork is cooking, combine jelly, mustard, and Madeira in a small heavy saucepan over moderately low heat. Bring to a boil, stirring occasionally. Continue cooking until sauce is smooth. Keep warm.

WHEN READY TO SERVE

Carve roast into thin slices and divide it among six dinner plates. Spoon about 2 tablespoons of Currant Sauce over each serving.

SEAFOOD

4 SERVINGS

*The boldness of the Cajun-spiced red snapper is tempered by the Lemon Butter Sauce.
It is an excellent entree to serve with lemon rice pilaf and Grilled Asparagus.*

2 teaspoons Cajun Magic Blackened Redfish
  Seasoning
2 Red Snapper filets (12 ounces each), halved

Lemon Butter Sauce

2 tablespoons fresh lemon juice
$\frac{1}{4}$ cup light margarine
1 tablespoon minced parsley

WHEN READY TO GRILL
Sprinkle $\frac{1}{2}$ teaspoon seasoning on each side of a red snapper filet. Over hot coals, place filets on a grill coated with nonstick vegetable spray. Cover grill and cook 4 minutes on each side.

To make Lemon Butter Sauce
While fish is cooking, bring lemon juice to a boil in a small saucepan over moderate heat. Remove pan from heat and add margarine; blend well. Add parsley just before serving.

WHEN READY TO SERVE
Spoon $1\frac{1}{2}$ tablespoons Lemon Butter Sauce over each blackened fish. Garnish with a sprig of parsley, if desired.

215 Calories
33.6 g Protein
0.7 g Carbohydrates
7.9 g Fat
33.0% Calories from Fat
0.0 g Fiber
440 mg Sodium
60 mg Cholesterol

4 SERVINGS

Ginger Oil and Ginger Sauce combine to subtly enhance the flavor of shark.
Serve with lemon rice pilaf and a blend of steamed carrots and zucchini.

Ginger Oil
½ cup extra-virgin olive oil
1 piece fresh ginger root, peeled and cut
   ¼ inch thick

Ginger Sauce
¼ cup sugar
1 can (14½ ounces) fat-free chicken broth
2 tablespoons chopped fresh ginger root

4 blackfin shark filets (5 ounces each)*
4 teaspoons ginger oil

*If shark is unavailable, substitute swordfish, marlin, or tuna.

196 Calories
21.3 g Protein
7.0 g Carbohydrates
8.8 g Fat
40.5% Calories from Fat
0.0 g Fiber
304 mg Sodium
50 mg Cholesterol

To make Ginger Oil

Combine oil and ginger root in a small heavy saucepan over moderate heat and bring to a boil. Remove saucepan from heat, cover, and let sit for 30 minutes. Pour Ginger Oil into a glass jar with a tight fitting lid and store in a dark, cool place. Use as needed. Makes ½ cup.

To make Ginger Sauce

Pour sugar into a small heavy saucepan over moderate heat for 5 to 6 minutes, or until the sugar begins to melt. Swirl the pan over the heat to melt sugar evenly. Add chicken broth and ginger root and cook over high heat for 8 to 10 minutes, or until the mixture is reduced to 1 cup. Keep Ginger Sauce warm until ready to serve.

WHEN READY TO GRILL

Brush each shark filet with ½ teaspoon Ginger Oil. Over hot coals, place shark filet, oiled side down, on a grill coated with nonstick vegetable spray. Brush top of each filet with ½ teaspoon Ginger Oil, cover grill, and cook 5 minutes on each side.

WHEN READY TO SERVE

Spoon about 2 tablespoons Ginger Sauce over each shark filet. Garnish each serving with a piece of slivered lemon peel.

4 SERVINGS

I use frozen lobster tail in this recipe because I have trouble dropping a live one into a pot of boiling water. (Of course, fresh lobster can be used as well.) Either way, grilled lobster combined with the Sesame Seed Dressing and condiments is fabulous!

WHEN READY TO SERVE
Place 1½ cups mixed greens on each dinner plate. Divide lobster among mixed greens and top with 2 tablespoons carrots, 2 tablespoons beets, and papaya. Drizzle 3 to 4 tablespoons dressing over each salad.

Sesame Seed Dressing
1 small garlic clove
1 tablespoon *each* tamari and sherry vinegar
½ teaspoon Dijon mustard
½ teaspoon sesame oil
½ cup canola oil

1 frozen lobster (1¼ pounds), thawed
   and cleaned
2 teaspoons extra-virgin olive oil

6 cups mixed greens
½ cup *each* julienned carrots and beets
1 large papaya, peeled and diced

To make dressing
In work bowl of food processor fitted with a metal blade, process garlic until chopped. Add tamari, sherry vinegar, mustard, and sesame oil and blend well. Add canola oil in a slow steady stream until well blended. Set aside.

WHEN READY TO GRILL
Brush each side of lobster with 1 teaspoon olive oil. Over hot coals, place lobster on a grill coated with nonstick vegetable spray. Cover grill and cook 12 to 14 minutes or until lobster is no longer translucent, turning lobster every 4 minutes. Remove shell and cut lobster into bite-size pieces.

385 Calories
19.5 g Protein
12.0 g Carbohydrates
29.5 g Fat
68.9% Calories from Fat
2.0 g Fiber
612 mg Sodium
59 mg Cholesterol

4 SERVINGS

This marinade is a quick and easy way to bring out the true flavors of marlin. It will also enhance the flavors of swordfish or sea bass. Serve with Grilled Ratatouille and steamed basmati rice.

Marinade

6 tablespoons fresh lemon juice

2 tablespoons extra-virgin olive oil

2 tablespoons *each* finely chopped parsley and
  green onion

1½ teaspoons *each* thyme and oregano

2 cloves garlic, minced

2 marlin filets (12 ounces each)

To make marinade

Combine lemon juice, olive oil, parsley, green onion, thyme, oregano, and garlic in a nonmetal dish. Add marlin and turn to coat both sides. Cover dish and refrigerate for 30 minutes.

WHEN READY TO GRILL

Over hot coals, place marlin on a grill coated with nonstick vegetable spray. Cover grill and cook 5 minutes on each side.

WHEN READY TO SERVE

Cut each marlin filet into 2 pieces. Garnish each serving with lemon wedges and a sprig of parsley.

267 Calories
37.6 g Protein
2.3 g Carbohydrates
11.3 g Fat
38.0% Calories from Fat
0.2 g Fiber
64 mg Sodium
61 mg Cholesterol

4 SERVINGS

This is a simple yet elegant way to serve salmon. Serve with lemon rice pilaf and a salad of baby greens dressed in a raspberry vinaigrette and accented with a small wedge of montrachet cheese.

¼ cup honey
3 tablespoons peppercorn mustard

1 salmon filet (24 ounces)

Combine honey and mustard in a small bowl.

WHEN READY TO GRILL
Brush honey and mustard mixture over top of salmon. Over hot coals, place salmon, skin side down, on a grill coated with nonstick vegetable spray. Cover grill and cook 10 to 12 minutes. Remove the skin and divide the salmon into four pieces.

316 Calories
33.3 g Protein
17.8 g Carbohydrates
11.9 g Fat
33.8% Calories from Fat
0.0 g Fiber
373 mg Sodium
90 mg Cholesterol

4 SERVINGS

*My husband loves hot and spicy food and these shrimp are among
his all-time favorites. Complement the meal with a first course of Louisiana
gumbo and serve the shrimp with white rice, French bread, and a glass of light beer.*

Marinade

½ cup fresh lemon juice
1 tablespoon extra-virgin olive oil
2 tablespoons freshly ground pepper
2 teaspoons rosemary
2 teaspoons Worcestershire sauce
1 teaspoon hot pepper sauce

2 pounds large shrimp

To make marinade

Combine lemon juice, olive oil, pepper, rosemary,
Worcestershire sauce, and hot pepper sauce in a nonmetal dish. Add shrimp (do not remove the shells) and
toss to coat. Cover dish and refrigerate 1 hour, turning
shrimp at least once.

WHEN READY TO GRILL

Place shrimp on skewers. Over hot coals, place shrimp on
a grill coated with nonstick vegetable spray. Cover grill
and cook 3 minutes on each side.

200 Calories
37.2 g Protein
3.3 g Carbohydrates
3.8 g Fat
16.9% Calories from Fat
0.1 g Fiber
412 mg Sodium
345 mg Cholesterol

SEA SCALLOP KEBABS

4 SERVINGS

*Sea scallops are members of the mollusk family and are
known for their two shells that are beautifully scalloped. The edible
part of the scallop is the abductor muscle, or eye, which opens and closes
the shells. Serve this delicious entree with steamed broccoli and a fresh fruit salad.*

WHEN READY TO GRILL

Place 6 to 8 scallops on each skewer. Over hot coals, place scallop kebabs on a grill coated with nonstick vegetable spray. Cover grill and cook 3 to 5 minutes on each side.

Marinade

¼ cup *each* rice wine and soy sauce
1 tablespoon sugar
1 piece fresh ginger root, peeled and cut
 ¼ inch thick

1½ pounds sea scallops

To make marinade

In a small saucepan over moderate heat, combine rice wine, soy sauce, sugar, and ginger root and blend well. Bring to a boil, lower heat, and simmer for 20 minutes, stirring occasionally. Remove ginger root. Allow marinade to come to room temperature. Use the marinade immediately or refrigerate in a covered container for up to 4 weeks.

Place scallops in a nonmetal dish and add ¼ cup marinade; turn scallops to coat both sides. Cover dish and refrigerate 45 minutes.

154 Calories
23.8 g Protein
9 6 g Carbohydrates
1.0 g Fat
6.1% Calories from Fat
0.0 g Fiber
1248 mg Sodium
45 mg Cholesterol

6 SERVINGS

The shrimp combine nicely with the Asian marinade and the flavor is heightened after grilling. Serve with Grilled Pears and herbed rice.

Marinade

¼ cup *each* rice wine and soy sauce

1 tablespoon sugar

1 piece fresh ginger root, peeled and cut
  ¼ inch thick

4 teaspoons sesame seeds

2 pounds large shrimp, peeled and deveined

To make marinade

In a small saucepan over moderate heat, combine rice wine, soy sauce, sugar, and ginger root and blend well. Bring to a boil, lower heat, and simmer for 20 minutes, stirring occasionally. Remove ginger root. Add sesame seeds and allow marinade to come to room temperature.

Place shrimp in a nonmetal dish and pour marinade over top; turn shrimp to coat pieces. Cover dish and refrigerate up to 2 hours.

WHEN READY TO GRILL

Place shrimp on skewers by alternating the direction the heads and tails face each other. Over hot coals, place shrimp on a grill coated with nonstick vegetable spray. Cover grill and cook 3 minutes on each side.

219 Calories
37.8 g Protein
6.5 g Carbohydrates
3.4 g Fat
13.9% Calories from Fat
0.1 g Fiber
653 mg Sodium
345 mg Cholesterol

4 SERVINGS

*The highly spiced salsa is a fusion of garlic, parsley,
and pepper. Its piquant tang balances the subtle flavor of the swordfish.
Serve with sautéed new potatoes and Grilled Asparagus.*

Garlic and Pepper Oil
½ cup extra-virgin olive oil
4 cloves garlic, minced
1 tablespoon freshly ground pepper

Parsley Salsa
½ cup parsley, tightly packed
2 cloves garlic
1 tablespoon capers
1 tablespoon Dijon mustard
2 tablespoons extra-virgin olive oil
¼ teaspoon *each* salt and freshly ground pepper

4 swordfish steaks (6 ounces each)
4 teaspoons Garlic and Pepper Oil

265 Calories
31.3 g Protein
1.1 g Carbohydrates
14.4 g Fat
48.9% Calories from Fat
0.2 g Fiber
287 mg Sodium
61 mg Cholesterol

To make Garlic and Pepper Oil

Combine olive oil, garlic, and pepper in a small heavy saucepan over moderate heat and bring to a boil. Remove saucepan from heat, cover, and let Garlic and Pepper Oil sit for 30 minutes. Pour Garlic and Pepper Oil into a glass jar with a tight-fitting lid and store in a dark, cool place. Use as needed. Makes ½ cup.

To make Parsley Salsa

In work bowl of food processor fitted with a metal blade, process parsley and garlic until finely chopped. Add capers, mustard, olive oil, salt, and pepper and process until smooth. Set aside.

WHEN READY TO GRILL

Brush each swordfish steak with ½ teaspoon Garlic and Pepper Oil. Over hot coals, place swordfish, oiled side down, on a grill coated with nonstick vegetable spray. Brush tops of each swordfish with ½ teaspoon Garlic and Pepper Oil, cover, and cook 5 to 6 minutes on each side.

WHEN READY TO GRILL

Place swordfish steaks on individual dinner plates and garnish each serving with a tablespoon of Parsley Salsa on the side.

4 SERVINGS

You will want to use this outstanding Honey Dijon Sauce with other kinds of grilled fish as well. Its sweet flavor delicately balances the smoky taste of the fish. Serve with grilled Pineapple Rings and stuffed zucchini.

WHEN READY TO SERVE

Remove ginger root from Honey Dijon Sauce. Place one shark steak on each dinner plate and spoon 2 tablespoons of sauce over each. Garnish each serving with chopped chives, if desired.

Honey Dijon Sauce

3 tablespoons *each* honey and plain nonfat yogurt
1 tablespoon hoisin sauce
1½ teaspoons *each* Dijon mustard and soy sauce
1½ tablespoons chopped chives
1 piece fresh ginger root, peeled and cut ¼ inch thick

8 teaspoons Ginger Oil (page 82)
4 shark steaks* (6 ounces each)

To make Honey Dijon Sauce

Combine honey, yogurt, hoisin sauce, mustard, soy sauce, chives, and ginger root in a small bowl. Set aside.

Soak 1 cup of your favorite smoking wood chips in water for 30 minutes.

WHEN READY TO GRILL

Place wet smoking chips on hot coals. Brush one side of each shark steak with 1 teaspoon Ginger Oil and place over coals, oiled side down, on a grill coated with nonstick vegetable spray. Brush top of each steak with 1 teaspoon Ginger Oil, cover grill, and cook 5 minutes on each side.

*If shark is unavailable, substitute tuna, salmon, or swordfish.**

345 Calories
29.1 g Protein
21.5 g Carbohydrates
15.8 g Fat
41.3% Calories from Fat
0.8 g Fiber
1001 mg Sodium
62 mg Cholesterol

VEGETABLES

4 SERVINGS

Asparagus never tasted so good!

1 pound asparagus
1 tablespoon extra-virgin olive oil
Dash of freshly ground white pepper

Snap off the ends of the asparagus. Place asparagus in a plastic bag and add olive oil. Roll asparagus in the olive oil until well coated.

WHEN READY TO GRILL
Over hot coals, place asparagus on a grilling grid coated with nonstick vegetable spray. Cover grill and cook 8 to 10 minutes, or until lightly browned, turning occasionally. Sprinkle asparagus with white pepper before serving.

43 Calories
1.5 g Protein
2.4 g Carbohydrates
3.6 g Fat
74.7% Calories from Fat
0.5 g Fiber
7 mg Sodium
0 mg Cholesterol

6 SERVINGS

*Whether you are a vegetarian or not, you will agree that this
savory dish is the highlight of any meal. The grilled vegetables mingle
perfectly with the spices and other ingredients to create a sensational flavor.
Serve on a bed of brown basmati rice and top with Raita (page 58).*

1 eggplant (½ pound), cut into ½-inch slices
10 new potatoes, halved
2 carrots, cut into 1½-inch chunks
1 crookneck squash, cut into 1½-inch chunks
1 Bermuda onion, cut into wedges
2 tablespoons extra-virgin olive oil
1 red pepper
⅔ cup apple juice
½ cup garbanzo beans
1 apple, peeled and cut into 1-inch chunks
½ cup raisins
1 tablespoon curry powder
¾ teaspoon cumin
½ teaspoon cinnamon

Sprinkle the eggplant with salt and place in a colander
for 30 minutes.

Place potatoes, carrots, squash, and onion in a plastic bag. Pour oil over vegetables and turn to coat pieces.
Place vegetables on skewers and set aside.

349 Calories
7.0 g Protein
71.6 g Carbohydrates
5.6 g Fat
14.4% Calories from Fat
5.5 g Fiber
36 mg Sodium
0 mg Cholesterol

WHEN READY TO GRILL

Over hot coals, place the red pepper on a grill coated with nonstick vegetable spray. Cover grill and cook 14 to 20 minutes, or until skin is charred all over, turning pepper as skin blackens. Place pepper in a plastic bag for 15 minutes. When the pepper is cool enough to handle, peel away the skin and remove the top and seeds (do not rinse the pepper). Cut the pepper into strips and set aside.

Place eggplant slices and vegetable skewers on grill. Cover grill and cook 10 to 12 minutes, turning vegetables every 3 minutes.

Remove skin and cut eggplant into cubes. Place eggplant, potatoes, carrots, squash, onion, red pepper, apple juice, garbanzo beans, apple, raisins, curry powder, cumin, and cinnamon in a large saucepan over moderate heat and blend well. Bring to a boil, reduce heat, cover, and simmer 7 to 10 minutes, or until heated through.

6 (1-CUP) SERVINGS

*The smoky accent from the grill in combination with the flavors
of the butternut squash, pear, and herbs is sensational in this versatile soup.
It can be enjoyed warm or cold. Serve with your favorite cornbread.*

1 butternut squash (1 pound)
1 pear, halved, seeds and stem removed
1 can (14½ ounces) fat-free chicken broth
1 medium onion, coarsely chopped
2 medium shallots, coarsely chopped
½ teaspoon thyme
¼ teaspoon *each* rosemary, salt, and freshly
    ground pepper
6 tablespoons skimmed evaporated milk
Lowfat sour cream (optional)
Chopped chives (optional)

Preheat oven to 325°

Cut squash in half and remove seeds. Place squash
on a baking sheet coated with vegetable spray and bake
for 35 minutes.

88 Calories
3.4 g Protein
18.9 g Carbohydrates
0.9 g Fat
9.1% Calories from Fat
4.2 g Fiber
406 mg Sodium
1 mg Cholesterol

WHEN READY TO GRILL

Over hot coals, place squash and pear halves on a grill coated with nonstick vegetable spray. Cover grill and cook 4 to 5 minutes on each side.

Scoop out flesh from squash and combine it in a large saucepan over moderately high heat with chicken broth, pear, onions, shallots, thyme, rosemary, salt, and pepper. Bring to a boil, cover, and simmer 20 minutes. Remove saucepan from heat and allow to sit for 10 minutes.

 Transfer soup mixture to work bowl of food processor fitted with a metal blade and process until pureed. Return soup mixture to saucepan and add evaporated milk, blending well. If serving hot, serve immediately and garnish each serving with a dollop of lowfat sour cream sprinkled with chopped chives, if desired. If serving the soup chilled, refrigerate, covered, for several hours or overnight.

EGGPLANT AND ZUCCHINI AU GRATIN

8 SERVINGS

*Grilling eggplant and zucchini enhances the true flavors of these vegetables.
In combination with roasted red peppers and onions, this becomes a truly savory
dish. Serve with grilled chicken or beef and a salad of mixed greens and tomatoes.*

2 eggplants (1 pound each), cut ½ inch thick
2 red peppers
4 tablespoons extra-virgin olive oil
2 zucchini (8 ounces each), halved
2 large onions, quartered
2 cloves garlic, minced
2 pounds tomatoes, cut ¼ inch thick and halved
½ teaspoon *each* thyme and savory
¼ teaspoon *each* salt and pepper
½ cup dry plain bread crumbs

Sprinkle eggplant slices with salt and place in a colander for 30 minutes.

149 Calories
3.0 g Protein
19.6 g Carbohydrates
7.7 g Fat
46.5% Calories from Fat
3.3 g Fiber
125 mg Sodium
0 mg Cholesterol

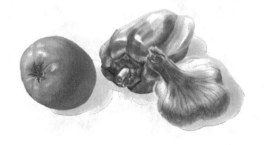

WHEN READY TO GRILL

Over hot coals, place the red peppers on a grill coated with vegetable spray. Cover grill and cook 14 to 20 minutes, or until skins are charred all over, turning peppers as skins blacken. Place the peppers in a plastic bag for 15 minutes. When peppers are cool enough to handle, peel away the skin and remove the top and seeds (do not rinse the peppers). Cut peppers into strips and set aside.

Pour 1 tablespoon olive oil into a plastic bag. Add eggplant slices and zucchini and turn to coat all over. Remove vegetables to a plate. Add 1 tablespoon olive oil to same bag and add onions; turn to coat.

Thread onions on skewers. Place eggplant slices, zucchini, and onions on grill. Cover grill and cook eggplant and zucchini 4 to 5 minutes on each side, or until brown and tender; cook onions for 10 to 12 minutes, turning onions every 4 minutes. Allow vegetables to cool for 10 minutes. Cut the eggplant into cubes and the zucchini and onions into ¼ inch thick slices.

Preheat oven to 350°.

Coat a small pan with nonstick vegetable spray and place over moderate heat. Add garlic and cook 2 to 3 minutes, stirring frequently. Combine garlic, red pepper, eggplant, and onions in an 8 × 11.5 × 2-inch oblong baking dish that has been coated with a nonstick vegetable spray and spread it evenly. Place an overlapping row of tomatoes over vegetables, starting at one short end of dish. Overlap a row of zucchini slices against tomatoes and continue this process with the remaining zucchini and tomato slices. Sprinkle the vegetables with thyme, savory, salt, and pepper and drizzle 1 tablespoon olive oil over all. Bake for 30 minutes. Remove eggplant au gratin from oven and top with bread crumbs and drizzle the last 1 tablespoon olive oil on top. Bake 15 minutes.

4 SERVINGS

*Florence fennel is a white bulbous root with heavy stalks
growing from the top that resemble celery. It has a wonderful anise
flavor and can be eaten both raw or cooked—grilling it is ideal!*

2 fennel
½ tablespoon extra-virgin olive oil

Trim the tops and remove the outer leaves and ends of
the fennel. Cut the fennel into quarters and thread them
onto skewers; brush with olive oil.

WHEN READY TO GRILL
Over hot coals, place fennel on a grill coated with nonstick
vegetable spray. Cover grill and cook 16 to 20 minutes, or
until brown and tender, turning every 3 minutes.

48 Calories
1.3 g Protein
7.6 g Carbohydrates
2.0 g Fat
37.1% Calories from Fat
1.7 g Fiber
54 mg Sodium
0 mg Cholesterol

4 SERVINGS

This fabulous recipe, featured in the Des Moines Register, *comes from Kingsford, a company known for a variety of charcoal briquettes and grilling accessories. Serve this salad with grilled lamb and warmed whole wheat pita pockets.*

¼ cup extra-virgin olive oil
1 tablespoon fresh lemon juice
2 teaspoons pressed garlic
1 teaspoon oregano
1 pound fresh vegetables (eggplant, assorted
   summer squash, bell peppers, mushrooms,
   and onions)

Combine olive oil, lemon juice, garlic, and oregano; set aside.

Slice eggplant into half-inch rounds. Cut small squash in half lengthwise; cut larger squash into ½-inch pieces. Cut bell peppers into large chunks. Slice mushrooms and cut onions into wedges or rounds. Toss vegetables with garlic oil to coat.

WHEN READY TO GRILL
Place vegetables in a single layer on grilling rack in covered grill over medium-hot coals. Grill 10 to 20 minutes, or until tender, turning once and basting with any remaining garlic oil. Remove vegetables as they become done and keep warm.

155 Calories
1.6 g Protein
7.9 g Carbohydrates
13.8 g Fat
80.3% Calories from Fat
1.6 g Fiber
3 mg Sodium
0 mg Cholesterol

8 SERVINGS

*This is a fabulous salad that combines the smoky flavor
of roasted red pepper, yellow squash, and Bermuda onions with a
Greek Salad Dressing and pasta. It can be served as the main course with
chunks of crusty French bread or try it as a side dish with grilled chicken.*

Greek Salad Dressing

1 clove garlic
2 tablespoons *each* fresh lemon juice and
    red wine vinegar
1 tablespoon oregano
½ teaspoon freshly ground pepper
5 tablespoons extra-virgin olive oil

Pasta

1 red pepper
1 crookneck squash, halved
1 tablespoon extra-virgin olive oil
1 Bermuda onion, peeled and quartered
12 ounces rigatoni
6 ounces fresh spinach, washed, dried, and torn
    into bite-size pieces
6 ounces feta cheese, crumbled
½ cup Greek olives, pitted and sliced

331 Calories
9.4 g Protein
35.9 g Carbohydrates
17.2 g Fat
46.7% Calories from Fat
4.1 g Fiber
388 mg Sodium
19 mg Cholesterol

To make Greek Salad Dressing

In work bowl of food processor fitted with a metal blade, process garlic until chopped. Add lemon juice, red wine vinegar, oregano, and pepper and process until combined. Add olive oil in a slow steady stream and process until well blended. Set aside.

WHEN READY TO GRILL

Over hot coals, place the red pepper on a grill coated with nonstick vegetable spray. Cover grill and cook 14 to 20 minutes or until skin is charred all over, turning pepper as skin blackens. Place pepper in a plastic bag for 15 minutes. When the pepper is cool enough to handle, peel away the skin and remove the top and the seeds (do not rinse the pepper). Cut pepper into thin strips and set aside.

Place crookneck squash on grill and brush with olive oil. Cover grill and cook 3 to 4 minutes on each side. Cut into thin slices. Set aside.

Thread Bermuda onion on a skewer and brush with olive oil. Place onion on grill and cook, covered, 10 to 12 minutes, turning every 3 minutes. Slice onion into slivers. Set aside.

Cook rigatoni according to package instructions. Drain well.

In a large bowl, combine rigatoni, red pepper, squash, onion, spinach, feta cheese, and olives and toss to blend. Add dressing and blend well. Serve at room temperature or refrigerate, covered, for several hours or overnight.

8 SERVINGS

The flavors of the grilled vegetables mingle perfectly with the herbs and spices as they bake together. Ratatouille can be a delicious appetizer spooned onto toast points, a side dish, even as a complete meal when served on a bed of steamed brown rice.

1 eggplant (1 pound), cut into ½-inch slices
3 tablespoons extra-virgin olive oil
1 zucchini, halved
1 crookneck squash, halved
1 onion, quartered
2 cloves garlic, minced
¼ cup chopped parsley
1 can (28 ounces) crushed tomatoes with
   tomato puree
1 teaspoon *each* basil and oregano
¼ teaspoon *each* salt and freshly ground pepper
¼ cup chopped fresh basil

Sprinkle salt over eggplant and place in a colander for 30 minutes.

Pour 2 tablespoons of the olive oil into a plastic bag. Add eggplant, zucchini, and squash and toss to coat all over. Remove vegetables to a plate. Add onions to the same bag and toss to coat. Place the onions on skewers.

103 Calories
2.3 g Protein
12.8 g Carbohydrates
5.6 g Fat
48.5% Calories from Fat
2.2 g Fiber
332 mg Sodium
0 mg Cholesterol

WHEN READY TO GRILL

Over hot coals place the vegetables on a grill coated with nonstick vegetable spray. Cover grill and cook eggplant, zucchini, and squash 4 to 5 minutes on each side and the onions for 10 to 12 minutes, turning onions every 4 minutes.

When vegetables are cool enough to handle, cut the eggplant into cubes and the zucchini, squash, and onion into slices.

In a large saucepan over moderate heat, cook the garlic in 1 tablespoon olive oil for 2 minutes. Add the eggplant, zucchini, squash, onions, parsley, tomatoes, 1 teaspoon dried basil, oregano, salt, and pepper and blend well. Cover saucepan and cook over moderately low heat for 30 minutes. Add ¼ cup fresh basil and blend well.

4 SERVINGS

The vegetables can be lightly brushed with olive oil before grilling; however, I prefer to make them with this flavorful marinade. Cold leftovers are delicious mixed with a little feta cheese and stuffed in pitas or tossed with warm pasta.

WHEN READY TO GRILL

Alternate squash, mushrooms, red pepper, onions, and eggplant onto skewers (reserving marinade). Over hot coals, place the vegetables on a grill coated with nonstick vegetable spray. Cover grill and cook 10 to 15 minutes, or until the vegetables are brown and tender, turning the skewers every 3 minutes and brushing with reserved marinade.

136 Calories
1.9 g Protein
9.5 g Carbohydrates
10.9 g Fat
72.2% Calories from Fat
1.7 g Fiber
103 mg Sodium
0 mg Cholesterol

Marinade

3 tablespoons extra-virgin olive oil
2 tablespoons *each* red wine vinegar and fresh lemon juice
1 tablespoon Dijon mustard
1 tablespoon *each* chopped fresh basil and parsley
1 large clove garlic, minced
$\frac{1}{8}$ teaspoon freshly ground pepper

Kebab Vegetables

1 small yellow squash, sliced $\frac{1}{4}$ inch thick
4 mushroom caps
1 red pepper, cut into 8 pieces
1 Bermuda onion, cut into chunks
1 Japanese eggplant, sliced $\frac{1}{4}$ inch thick

To make marinade

Combine olive oil, red wine vinegar, lemon juice, mustard, basil, parsley, garlic, and pepper in a 1-gallon reclosable plastic bag. Add squash, mushrooms, red pepper, onion, and eggplant and toss to coat vegetables. Refrigerate 2 to 3 hours.

4 SERVINGS

Yams are perfect for grilling. They are sweeter and larger than sweet potatoes and their skin is usually purplish or reddish brown in color rather than orange.

1½ tablespoons extra-virgin olive oil
4 yams, sliced ½ inch thick

WHEN READY TO GRILL
Pour olive oil into a plastic bag and add yams; turn to coat all over. Over hot coals, place yams on a grill coated with nonstick vegetable spray. Cover grill and cook 10 minutes on each side, or until brown and tender.

203 Calories
2.0 g Protein
37.5 g Carbohydrates
5.3 g Fat
23.5% Calories from Fat
4.1 g Fiber
11 mg Sodium
0 mg Cholesterol

4 SERVINGS

*This pizza is definitely a favorite among my children and their friends.
The naan (Indian bread) is the perfect size for making individual size pizzas
and it makes a wonderful crispy crust when cooked on the grill and topped
with the cheese and vegetables. Naan is available in most Asian food stores.*

4 teaspoons extra-virgin olive oil
4 naan breads
1½ cups skimmed milk mozzarella cheese
4 teaspoons minced garlic
1 large yellow pepper, seeded and thinly sliced
1 large tomato, thinly sliced
1 small bunch broccoli florets, parboiled 1 minute
    and thinly sliced*
1½ cups skimmed milk mozzarella cheese

*This pizza can be made with any of your favorite vegetables.

443 Calories
28.2 g Protein
34.2 g Carbohydrates
22.3 g Fat
45.2% Calories from Fat
3.4 g Fiber
439 mg Sodium
48 mg Cholesterol

Brush 1 teaspoon oil on a naan and sprinkle 6 table-spoons cheese, 1 teaspoon garlic, and one fourth of the yellow pepper, tomato, and broccoli slices all over; top with 6 tablespoons cheese. Repeat this process with the remaining naan.

WHEN READY TO GRILL
Prepare grill with charcoal on only one half of the grill and place an aluminum pan on the empty side. When coals are hot, place a prepared pizza over coals on a grill coated with nonstick vegetable spray. Cover grill and cook 1 minute. Using a very wide spatula or tongs, move pizza directly over the aluminum pan and away from the coals. Cover grill and cook 10 minutes, or until cheese has melted and vegetables are heated through. Prepare remaining 3 pizzas in the same way.

8 SERVINGS

*These veggie burgers are chock-full of wholesome vegetables
and grains. They are wonderful topped with lettuce, thinly sliced Vidalia onions,
tomatoes, green pepper, and alfalfa sprouts and nestled in whole-wheat buns.*

½ cup bulgur
¾ cup boiling water
½ cup water
¼ cup quinoa
4 shallots
1 can (19 ounces) cannelloni beans, drained
1 cup bread crumbs
¾ cup packed chopped fresh spinach
½ cup chopped carrots
¼ cup packed chopped parsley
2 tablespoons *each* chopped celery and walnuts
2 mushrooms, chopped
½ tablespoon Worcestershire sauce
½ teaspoon freshly ground pepper

164 Calories
7.2 g Protein
31.1 g Carbohydrates
1.7 g Fat
9.2% Calories from Fat
4.3 g Fiber
279 mg Sodium
1 mg Cholesterol

Place bulgur in a large mixing bowl and pour ¾ cup boiling water over it. Let sit for 15 minutes. Transfer bulgur to a sieve and drain well. Push down on the bulgur with a spoon to remove as much water as possible. Return bulgur to mixing bowl and set aside.

In a small saucepan, bring ½ cup water to a boil over moderately high heat. Add quinoa, reduce heat, cover, and cook 20 minutes. Add quinoa to bulgur.

In work bowl of food processor fitted with a metal blade, process shallots until finely chopped. Add cannelloni beans and puree. Add bread crumbs, spinach, carrots, parsley, celery, walnuts, mushrooms, Worcestershire sauce, and pepper and blend well. Form the mixture into 8 veggie burgers.

WHEN READY TO GRILL

Over hot coals, place burgers on grill coated with nonstick vegetable spray. Cover grill and cook 8 to 12 minutes, turning burgers every 3 minutes.

4 SERVINGS

Portobello mushrooms are giant, cultivated mushrooms that are dark brown in color and have an open cap. They are delicious combined with garlicky sauce and pasta. Serve with crusty bread.

Garlic Sauce

1 cup loosely packed parsley
2 green onions, cut into 2-inch pieces
3 cloves garlic
1 tablespoon white wine vinegar
1 teaspoon thyme
¼ teaspoon *each* salt and freshly ground pepper
¼ cup extra-virgin olive oil

1 red pepper
1 package ziti (16 ounces)
10 ounces Portobello mushrooms, sliced
   ½ inch thick
1 tablespoon extra-virgin olive oil
1½ tablespoons parmesan cheese

587 Calories
16.5 g Protein
86.4 g Carbohydrates
19.8 g Fat
30.4% Calories from Fat
9.6 g Fiber
183 mg Sodium
2 mg Cholesterol

To make Garlic Sauce

In work bowl of food processor fitted with metal blade, process parsley, green onions, and garlic until finely chopped. Add white wine vinegar, thyme, salt, and pepper and process until blended. Add olive oil in a slow steady stream and process until well blended. Set aside.

WHEN READY TO GRILL

Over hot coals, place the red pepper on a grill. Cover grill and cook pepper 14 to 20 minutes, or until skin is charred all over, turning pepper as skin blackens. Place pepper in a plastic bag for 15 minutes. When pepper is cool enough to handle, peel away the skin and remove the top and seeds (do not rinse the pepper). Cut the pepper into strips and set aside.

Cook ziti according to package directions, drain, and keep warm.

While ziti is cooking, place mushroom slices on skewers and brush with olive oil. Over hot coals, place mushrooms on a grill coated with nonstick vegetable spray. Cover grill and cook mushrooms 5 minutes on each side. Cut mushrooms into thin slices.

Place ziti, pepper, mushrooms, and parmesan cheese in a large serving bowl. Pour Garlic Sauce over pasta mixture and blend well.

MAKES 2 CUPS

When I was very young, my mother made a dish similar to this called "poor man's caviar." She baked the eggplant in the oven; however, I prefer to make it on the grill so the eggplant picks up a smoky flavor. Serve with cut-up pita bread or crackers.

1 eggplant (1 pound)
1 tablespoon toasted sesame seeds
6 green onions
3 tablespoons minced parsley
3 cloves garlic, minced
3 tablespoons fresh lemon juice
¼ cup tahini*
1 tablespoon *each* soy sauce and honey
1 tablespoon extra-virgin olive oil
⅛ teaspoon salt

*Tahini is made from ground, roasted sesame seeds and has the consistency of peanut butter. It is available in most health food stores.

48 Calories
1.2 g Protein
4.6 g Carbohydrates
3.1 g Fat
59.3% Calories from Fat
0.8 g Fiber
85 mg Sodium
0 mg Cholesterol

Cut eggplant into ¼-inch thick slices and lightly sprinkle both sides with salt. Place eggplant slices in a colander for 30 minutes.

Preheat oven to 350°.

Place sesame seeds in a small pan and bake 10 to 15 minutes, or until golden brown. Set aside.

WHEN READY TO GRILL

Over hot coals, place eggplant slices on a grill coated with nonstick vegetable spray. Cover grill and cook eggplant 5 to 6 minutes on both sides, or until brown and tender. Allow the eggplant to come to room temperature before removing skin. Set aside.

In work bowl of food processor fitted with a metal blade, process onions, parsley, and garlic until finely chopped. Add eggplant and process until blended. Add lemon juice, tahini, soy sauce, honey, sesame seeds, olive oil, and salt and process until smooth. Refrigerate spicy eggplant dip in a covered container for several hours or overnight.

FRUITS

4 SERVINGS

Choose firm apples so they retain their shape even over the heat of the grill.

4 apples, cored

WHEN READY TO GRILL
Cut apples into ½-inch slices and remove any seeds. Over hot coals, place apples on a grilling grid coated with non-stick vegetable spray. Cover grill and cook 4 to 5 minutes on each side, or until apples are golden brown and tender.

77 Calories
0.3 g Protein
20.0 g Carbohydrates
0.5 g Fat
5.8% Calories from Fat
2.9 g Fiber
1 mg Sodium
0 mg Cholesterol

GRILLED BANANAS

4 SERVINGS

These bananas are delicious when served with grilled meats or poultry. They also become part of a delicious dessert served alongside of frozen fat-free yogurt.

4 bananas
3 tablespoons light margarine, melted

WHEN READY TO GRILL
Remove banana peel and cut bananas in half lengthwise. Brush each side with melted margarine. Over hot coals, place bananas on a grilling grid coated with nonstick vegetable spray. Cover grill and cook bananas 4 to 5 minutes on each side, or until golden brown.

143 Calories
1.2 g Protein
26.7 g Carbohydrates
4.8 g Fat
30.2% Calories from Fat
1.8 g Fiber
105 mg Sodium
0 mg Cholesterol

FRUIT KEBABS

4 SERVINGS

Grilling the fresh fruit adds a wonderful smoky flavor that balances the sweetness of the fruit. These fruit kebabs make a delightful accompaniment to grilled chicken or pork or can be served as a dessert with a dish of fat-free frozen yogurt.

8 strawberries, hulled
2 bananas, cut into 8 chunks
2 kiwis, peeled and cut into 8 slices
8 (1-inch) cubes cantaloupe
8 (1-inch) cubes fresh pineapple

¼ cup pineapple juice

Soak 8 bamboo skewers in water for at least 30 minutes or overnight.

WHEN READY TO GRILL
Alternate strawberries, banana, kiwi, cantaloupe, and pineapple among the skewers. Brush the fruit with pineapple juice. Over medium-hot coals, place the skewers on a grill coated with nonstick vegetable spray. Cover grill and cook 6 to 8 minutes, turning skewers every 3 minutes and brushing with pineapple juice.

106 Calories
1.4 g Protein
26.5 g Carbohydrates
0.7 g Fat
5.9% Calories from Fat
3.1 g Fiber
5 mg Sodium
0 mg Cholesterol

4 SERVINGS

*Like many grilled fruits, peaches make a wonderful
accompaniment to poultry or pork and can double as a dessert.*

4 firm peaches, peeled, cut in half, pit removed

WHEN READY TO GRILL
Over medium-hot coals, place peaches on a grill coated
with nonstick vegetable spray. Cover grill and cook 4 to
5 minutes on each side, or until golden brown.

35 Calories
0.6 g Protein
9.2 g Carbohydrates
0.1 g Fat
2.6% Calories from Fat
1.3 g Fiber
0 mg Sodium
0 mg Cholesterol

GRILLED PEARS

4 SERVINGS

This versatile fruit can complement a savory serving of pork or be served unadorned as a simple dessert.

4 firm pears, halved, cored, and seeded

WHEN READY TO GRILL
Over medium-hot coals, place pears on a grilling grid coated with nonstick vegetable spray. Cover grill and cook 4 to 5 minutes on each side, or until golden brown.

93 Calories
0.6 g Protein
23.8 g Carbohydrates
0.6 g Fat
5.8% Calories from Fat
4.1 g Fiber
1 mg Sodium
0 mg Cholesterol

4 SERVINGS

Grilling adds a subtle smoky flavor to this traditional accompaniment to fish or ham.

1 whole pineapple

Using a sharp knife, remove top and bottom of pineapple. With a pineapple cutter or a very sharp knife, remove outer skin and core. Slice pineapple into ½-inch slices.

WHEN READY TO GRILL
Over medium-hot coals, place pineapple slices on a grilling grid coated with nonstick vegetable spray. Cover grill and cook pineapple 4 to 6 minutes on each side, or until golden brown.

88 Calories
0.7 g Protein
21.9 g Carbohydrates
0.8 g Fat
8.2% Calories from Fat
2.1 g Fiber
2 mg Sodium
0 mg Cholesterol

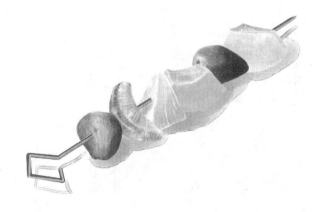